Cultivating Reading and Phonics Skills
1st Grade – 3rd Grade

Instruction Manual for Teachers and Parents of Children with Dyslexia, Dysgraphia, ADHD, and Other Learning Challenges

Laurie Hunter

Illustrations by Gabrielle Watson

Published by Laurie Hunter
Austin, TX

Copyright © 2020 Laurie Hunter
Derivative works: Teach Your Child to Read©2013, and Mosaic Reading©2004

Books by Laurie Hunter
Cultivating Reading and Phonics Skills 1st Grade – 3rd Grade
Phonics Stories - Short Vowels - Level 1
Phonics Stories - Long Vowels - Level 2
Phonics Stories - The Other Vowel Sounds - Level 3
Phonics Stories - Advanced Long and Short Vowel Patterns - Level 4
Cultivating Respect and Cooperation in the Classroom and at Home

All rights reserved. This book may not be reproduced in whole or in part, or transmitted in any form, without written permission from the publisher, except by a reviewer who may quote brief passages in a review; nor may any part of this book be reproduced, stored in a retrieval system, or transmitted in any form or by any means electronic, mechanical, photocopying, recording, or other,
without written permission from the publisher.
For inquiries and to obtain permission, please submit a written request to
Laurie Hunter, 9009 Corran Ferry Dr. Austin, TX 78749
www.lauriehunter.org

Library of Congress Publisher's Cataloging-in-Publication Data
Publisher's Cataloging-in-Publication Data

Names: Hunter, Laurie, 1969- author.
Title: Cultivating reading and phonics skills, 1st grade - 3rd grade : an instruction manual for teachers and parents of children with dyslexia, dysgraphia, ADHD, and other learning challenges / Laurie Hunter.
Description: Austin, TX : Laurie Hunter, 2020. | Includes bibliographical references.
Identifiers: LCCN 2020921879 (print) | ISBN 978-0-9974882-2-7 (paperback) | ISBN 978-0-9974882-7-2 (ebook)
Subjects: LCSH: Reading--Phonetic method. | Reading (Elementary) | Reading--Phonetic method--Study and teaching. | Language arts--Handbooks, manuals, etc. | Learning disabilities--Handbooks, manuals, etc. | English language. | BISAC: EDUCATION / Teaching / Subjects / Reading & Phonics. | EDUCATION / Teaching / Subjects / Language Arts. | EDUCATION / Special Education / Learning Disabilities.
Classification: LCC LB1050.34 .H86 2020 (print) | LCC LB1050.34 (ebook) | DDC 372.46/5--dc23.

Publisher: Laurie Hunter
Cover Design: Pixelstudio
Cover Art: Ping198/Shutterstock.com
Interior Illustrations: Gabrielle Watson
Interior Design: Codrut Sebastian Fagaras

TABLE OF CONTENTS

ACKNOWLEDGMENTS — vii

HOW TO USE THIS INSTRUCTION MANUAL — ix

INTRODUCTION — 1

STEP 1 | TEACH SHORT VOWELS AND THEIR SOUNDS — 11

STEP 2 | TEACH CONSONANTS AND THEIR SOUNDS — 27

STEP 3 | PROVIDE PRACTICE BLENDING SOUNDS TO MAKE WORDS — 59

STEP 4 | TEACH LONG VOWELS AND THEIR SOUNDS — 96

STEP 5 | EXPLAIN SOFT C AND G — 129

STEP 6 | TEACH *THE OTHER* VOWEL SOUNDS — 135

STEP 7 | TEACH ADVANCED LONG AND SHORT VOWEL PATTERNS — 163

STEP 8 | SUPPORT READING AND SPELLING WITH SOUND AWARENESS — 209

APPENDIX A: Beginning, Middle, End — 214

APPENDIX B: 3-D Flash Cards — 215

REFERENCES — 251

LAURIE HUNTER

For Preston, Warren, and Samantha

ACKNOWLEDGMENTS

My deepest thanks go to my family, especially Jeff, Preston, Warren, and Samantha. Much gratitude goes to my husband and all my parents. Thank you for understanding my mission and being supportive. I am most grateful to my three children, my first teachers of dyslexia and ADHD. Thank you for letting me work with you, learn from you, and be inspired by you.

I'd also like to thank all the tutors, especially Laura Pittman, Teresa Flores, Carla Trautwein and Wendy Taylor. Thanks for your hard work and dedication to helping our youth succeed and for encouraging me to get this instruction manual into the hands of others! Laura, thank you for asking me to speak up and advocate for your daughter and other children. Because of that, we have created shifts in mentalities that improved the outcomes of dyslexic children and success in school. You are a loving mother who learned as much as you could to teach your daughter and other children as well. That made an impression on me. Seeing your love in action made me realize how many other parents would like to do the same, if only they knew what to do.

Many thanks go to my teachers, especially Rebecca Everett and Dr. Hougen. I can't imagine what my children's lives would be like without your help. Both of you have taught me and helped me improve my children's lives in a way I will always remember and appreciate.

Much gratitude goes to the parents of my students, especially Dawn Piper, Cathy Humphrey, Madeline Mansen, and Janel Hester. Thanks for being so supportive, determined, and courageous when it came to advocating for your children. I witnessed what a mother's love can do. You and your children are an inspiration.

I can't thank my students enough, each and every one of you. Thank you for your hard work and effort. I admired your determination. You developed strong work ethics and achieved success that you can be proud of. You are all my heroes.

And most of all, I thank God for blessing me with dyslexia. Because of my dyslexia, You've given me insight and a deep understanding of my children and my students. Because of my dyslexia, You've blessed me with visual and problem-solving abilities that helped me create a reading program that effectively addresses the needs of struggling readers and spellers. Thank You for blessing me with three dyslexic/ADHD children. Because of them, You've given me what it takes to help other parents of students who experience difficulties

CULTIVATING READING AND PHONICS SKILLS 1ST GRADE – 3RD GRADE

with reading, spelling, and written expression. And because of the experiences, obstacles, and challenges You've placed before me, I have come to know nothing is too great, and anything is possible.

HOW TO USE THIS INSTRUCTION MANUAL

This instruction manual is for parents, tutors, and teachers who want to provide reading intervention to students who are experiencing difficulties learning to read.

The methods in this manual are appropriate for students with any of the following characteristics:

- Nonreaders of any age, beginning readers, and students reading below grade-level
- Students who have dyslexia, dysgraphia, ADHD, orthographic processing challenges, and autism
- English language learners

This manual is appropriate for use in the following environments: Special Education, Gifted and Talented programs, general education classrooms, tutoring programs, and homeschool.

This intervention is not intended to replace students' daily Language Arts classroom instruction. Rather, it is to be provided in addition to students' regular Language Arts curriculum.

Previous experience is not required using this method, because teachers, tutors, and parent instructors will learn along with the student.

To ensure optimal results, instructors should:

1) Read through each step before working on it with students.

2) Work on one step at a time and in the order they are presented in this manual.

Strategies in each unit are cumulative and should be practiced throughout the program.

INTRODUCTION

> "*To avoid criticism, do nothing, say nothing, be nothing.*"
>
> Aristotle

First grade was dreadful for my twin sons, Preston and Warren. They would cry every day, begging to stay home from school. By the end of the school year their teachers and principal insisted that they repeat 1st grade because "they needed more time to mature." I didn't know then that they had dyslexia. But I did know that another year of the same instruction was not the answer. I pleaded with the school to allow me to work with them over the summer before automatically retaining them. They agreed but said that they would reassess the boys' skills when school started in the fall. They warned me that, if my sons could not meet second-grade expectations, they would not be promoted on to the second grade.

It was then that I began my research on reading difficulties. I knew that I had to do something other than make my sons read more. Because the more I forced them to read, the more it made them, *and me,* anxious and frustrated. I found that there were no practical books for the proactive parent wanting to teach their child how to read, write, and spell. And even though I found numerous books about dyslexia, they provided only vague descriptions of activities parents could do with their children. I wanted to know what activities *truly* fostered the skills needed when learning to read. I decided that I would teach them phonics and in a way that made sense to me.

We worked hard that summer and, in the fall, the school reassessed my sons and they were both promoted on to the second grade. That school year, I continued to work with them and hired a reading tutor. She taught me how to effectively communicate with my children's teachers, counselor, and principal. She also inspired me to insist that a reluctant school test my sons for dyslexia and to advocate for my children.

After my sons were tested for dyslexia, their school could not provide them with intervention for dyslexia, so I offered to tutor them myself at their school during school hours. I offered my services to other students as well. By the end of the year, I worked with 25 students at my sons' school and nine others at a neighboring school. I recruited and trained 13 parent volunteers to tutor the 34 students. It was a grassroots, parent-volunteer effort to support teachers in providing intervention to dyslexic students and other struggling readers.

CULTIVATING READING AND PHONICS SKILLS 1ST GRADE – 3RD GRADE

I think back and remember how I felt when I realized that my sons had dyslexia. I was optimistic because knowing meant that I could finally find out what the *true* problems were and address the *root causes* of their issues. That seemed to give me more peace than crossing my fingers, waiting for them to "mature," or waiting for "the lightbulb to come on." Over these years, I have tutored Pre-K through high-school students who were nonreading, reading below grade-level, English language learners with dyslexia, ADHD, autism, and other learning challenges. I have come to understand that just because a child has any of those characteristics, it does not sentence him or her to a life of not being able to read, write, or spell. On the contrary, proper intervention and an active parent can make a huge difference in the academic success of a child.

I may have taught my three children how to read, but they have taught me so much more. They have taught me that *in what may seem like an overwhelming and powerless situation we, parents, have more control than we can imagine*. When I began working with my children, I was not a teacher. Nor did I have a degree in education. I was just a parent who wanted to stop the tears. I got so much more. If I could do it, then any parent, teacher, or tutor can also...whether your child or student has dyslexia or simply is having a difficult time learning to read.

All three of my children started their academic careers with challenges. I was not a reading specialist then; I was merely a mom who wanted to do whatever I could to turn around their unsuccessful introductions to school. Since then, they have become academic successes. I've received my Master's in Education and I specialize in providing instruction and interventions to children with blends of characteristics, such as dyslexia, ADHD, English Language Learner, Special Education, and/or Gifted and Talented.

Current reading programs contain an overwhelming amount of content. I understand the time constraints and emotional needs of struggling students, parents, and teachers, I've chosen the most essential information, strategies, and techniques that will have the most significant impact on your child(ren).

My experience with my children and students over the years has also taught me that the human spirit is tenacious in getting what it wants. So dear reader, roll up your sleeves, we've got a lot of work to do.

UNDERSTAND THE PROCESS OF LEARNING TO READ

When your child or student is struggling with reading, you can be a more effective influence if you are aware of the mechanics involved in learning how to read and where breakdowns can occur. This insight can help you work with your child, improve communication with teachers and principals, and advocate for your child.

Reading problems can stem from difficulties such as decoding, phonemic awareness, orthographic processing, fluency, comprehension. All these skills are related and students can experience problems in one or more of these as well as other areas.

For a beginner reader, decoding is the process that involves recognizing letters and letter groups, and in understanding the phonemes (sounds) they can make. Phonemes are the smallest parts of speech. For example, even though there are 5 letters in the word *shell*, it contains only three phonemes, /sh/ /e/ /l/. English consists of about 41 phonemes (sounds). When decoding words, students blend phonemes to read words.

More specifically, new readers decode by sounding out the first letter or letter group, converting it to its corresponding speech sound (sound-symbol correspondence). Next, they move to the right (directionality) and blend the first sound with the next sound (blending). Then they continue in the same manner with the following sounds. Beginner readers repeat those sounds at the rate of speech to hear the word. When the sound-symbol correspondence, directionality, and blending are performed automatically then automaticity is achieved (Hallahan et al, 2005). Difficulties in these areas can affect decoding (sounding out), comprehension (understanding), and reading fluency (rate and accuracy).

UNDERSTAND THE ROOT CAUSES OF READING DIFFICULTIES

Decoding, phonemic awareness, reading fluency, and comprehension are all related. Problems in any of these areas affect reading and comprehension abilities.

Figure 1.1   Skills Needed for Beginning Readers to Decode Words

Phonemic Awareness (Awareness of the Sounds that Letters and Letter Groups Make) **+** **Phonic Knowledge** (Letter-Sound Knowledge) **=** **Effective Decoding Skills** (Accurate and Automatic Sounding Out)

Phonemic awareness is not phonics. Rather, it is the ability to hear, identify, and manipulate the individual sounds in words (Eunice Kennedy Shriver NICHHD, 2001, p 1). "Effective phonemic awareness instruction teaches children to notice, think about, and work with (manipulate) sounds in spoken language" (p 4). "**Phonics** instruction teaches children the relationships between the letters (graphemes) of written language and the individual sounds (phonemes) of spoken language" (p 11).

CULTIVATING READING AND PHONICS SKILLS 1ST GRADE – 3RD GRADE

It is important to note that the difference between skilled and unskilled beginner readers is not an issue of intelligence or motivation. The difference lies in how well a child can break down words into phonic chunks and convert those chunks into sounds.

Problems with Phonemic Awareness and Phonics Affect Reading Fluency and Comprehension

The National Reading Panel (NRP) issued a report in 2000, titled *Teaching Children to Read*, in response to a mandate by Congress. The panel reviewed 100,000 studies examining the effectiveness of reading instruction for struggling readers in kindergarten through third grade. The report identifies essential components of reading instruction: phonemic awareness, phonics, fluency, vocabulary, and text comprehension. The panel's analysis concluded that *systematic* and *explicit* phonics instruction significantly improves word recognition, spelling, and reading comprehension for kindergarten and first grade students (Eunice Kennedy Shriver NICHHD, 2001).

Readers who struggle with decoding will consequently struggle with reading fluency. Reading fluency is the ability to read swiftly, accurately, and with expression. A dysfluent reader reads slower, sounds choppy, pauses more frequently, reads fewer correct words per minute (CWPM), and lacks expression while reading. While reading, a dysfluent reader requires time and energy to read words, making it more challenging for the reader to get meaning out of what was read and hence, correlates with low comprehension in the elementary grades.

Figure 1.2 Reading Skills that Influence Reading Fluency and Comprehension

Poor Reading Skills Impact Reading Proficiency	Behavior
Poor Phonemic Awareness and Phonic Knowledge ⬇ Difficulty Converting Letters to Speech Sounds ⬇ Poor Decoding Skills ⬇ Poor Word Recognition ⬇ Poor Reading Fluency / Poor Reading Vocabulary ⬇ Poor Comprehension	Lack of Success in Reading Skills ⬇ Limited Academic, Social, and Emotional Competencies (such as coping with frustration and anxiety) ⬇ Poor Behavior, Grades, and Self-Confidence

PROVIDE EFFECTIVE READING INTERVENTION

This manual can be used to provide reading instruction to any student who is a nonreader, experiencing difficulty learning to read, or is reading below their grade-level. It can also be used to provide reading intervention to students who have orthographic processing difficulties, dyslexia, ADHD, autism, or is an English Language Learner, in Special Education, or is behind due to poor academic instruction at school. This method has the following basic characteristics shown to improve the reading proficiency of struggling readers.

Explicitly and Systematically Introduce Letters and Letter Groups with Their Sounds

The importance of providing phonics instruction that is explicit and systematic has been widely documented. Explicit phonics programs teach phonics rules, point out relationships, and do not leave it to students to implicitly figure out patterns. When phonics is taught systematically, then phonics patterns are introduced in a carefully selected and logical order. If reading instruction is not explicit and systematic, then it can be extremely difficult for children with learning differences to learn how to accurately decode (read).

Figure 1.3 Instruction for Students with Learning Differences

Students with learning challenges require instruction that is:

Systematic – teach phonics and blending in an orderly and methodical way

Direct – teach word study in a way that is straightforward and to the point

Explicit – teach phonics in a way that is clearly stated, nothing is implied

Cumulative – introduce new material with previously learned material for mastery

Combine Phonemic Awareness with Phonics Instruction

When new readers learn how to read with a program that combines phonics instruction (letters/letter groups) with phonemic awareness practice (letters with sounds), the program benefits all students of all abilities. Their are different types of phonics instruction. The NRP meta-analysis found synthetic phonics to be the most effective (Eunice Kennedy Shriver NICHHD, 2001). Synthetic phonics teaches students to convert letters and letter groups into sounds and to blend the sounds to recognizable words (Hallahan, p 387).

CULTIVATING READING AND PHONICS SKILLS 1ST GRADE – 3RD GRADE

Use a Multisensory Approach to Help Students Build Sound-Symbol Relationships

Multisensory approaches use visual, auditory, kinesthetic, and tactile (VAKT) senses during reading, spelling, and writing instruction. Gillingham and Stillman created a multisensory program based on the work of Samuel T. Orton in the 1930's to remediate students' difficulties in reading, spelling, and handwriting. The Orton-Gillingham approach teaches the letters, letter groups, and their sounds whereby the student sees a letter (visual), says and hears its sound (auditory), and writes it (kinesthetic). Other Orton-Gillingham-based approaches include Slingerland (Lovitt & DeMier, 1984), Wilson (Wilson, 2002), and Alphabetic Phonics (Ogden, Hindman, & Turner, 1989) and many others.

Provide Practice Blending Letters, Letter Groups, and Syllables

Although there is plentiful research-based evidence stating that teaching the alphabetic principle is critical to the prevention of and intervention for learning disabilities, presently there is less evidence regarding strategies for blending, an important aspect of the alphabetic principle. The Open Court reading program has a specific way of teaching blending. For example, to blend the sounds in the word *ran*, the child is taught to focus on the initial sound (/r/) and the medial sound (/a/), then to combine them (/ra/) before saying the final sound (/n/) to produce the entire word /ran/ (Rayner, 2001, p 58).

Figure 1.4 Cultivating Reading and Phonics Skills

This Intervention Addresses:

Explicit and Systematic Phonics Instruction

Phonics Combined with Phonemic and Phonological Awareness Exercises

Multisensory Techniques and Memory Strategies

Practice Blending Letters and Letter Groups

Handwriting and Spelling Exercises that Mirror the Phonic Patterns Learned

Interactive Responses to Confirm Student's Knowledge and Provide Corrective Feedback

Confidence Building

If a school is reluctant or cannot provide intervention to students who are reading below grade level, parents/teachers should advocate for children to receive proper reading instruction that will effectively increase their reading, spelling, and writing proficiency. Parents, teachers, and tutors can use this manual to supply their children with effective intervention at home or in school settings. Parents, teachers, and tutors can also use this manual to provide intervention in addition to what the school provides.

DEVELOP CONFIDENCE

Severe reading difficulty takes a toll on self-confidence. Encouragement and support should be provided to any young student experiencing a difficulty in learning to read. Address confidence in as many ways as you can.

Build Reading Confidence

- Assist the student in setting realistic and attainable goals, one after the other.
- Teach that a person cannot reach a destination in a single step. Ask the student to imagine walking from one side of the room to the other in one step. Explain that every journey is made up of many steps and that we cannot reach our destination in the first step.
- During each session, comment on one small success after another.
- After each session, briefly rejoice and relish the student's accomplishments.
- At the end of each unit, give the student an opportunity to browse through his or her work. It is motivating to see one's progress.

Prevent Feelings of Failure to Preserve and Maintain Confidence

- Don't ask a student to go too far beyond his or her ability.
- Don't skip steps. Don't skip activities. If you think an activity will be too easy, have the student go through it anyway. If it is easy, then it won't take much of your time and most importantly, it will build confidence within the student.

If the Student Fails, Restore Confidence

- Respect the student's dignity.
- Quickly follow up by placing them in a situation where you know they will succeed.
- Establish the FACT that we all learn from our mistakes.

Patience, patience, patience. When times are challenging, think about how you would feel if you were failing miserably at your job. Say you couldn't switch jobs; you had to make it work. How would you want your boss to treat you? How would you feel if he or she yelled at you? Would it motivate you to do better? What words would you need to hear? Write the answers on notepaper and place it where you can glance at it when you're working with your student(s).

Think about your role as an instructor to be much like an artist making a tile mosaic. You would plan your work before you lay down the first tile, right? So always prepare before sitting down with your student!

CULTIVATING READING AND PHONICS SKILLS 1ST GRADE – 3RD GRADE

You wouldn't throw down multiple tiles at once, you would lay down one tile at a time, so teach each lesson one at a time and in order. An artist would also adhere the tiles together with care, so make sure the "cement" is adequate, so the lessons connect to each other and the information sticks.

Finally, you would polish your mosaic so the beauty of the pieces can show their brilliance. In the same way, take care to develop your children's self-confidence while they are working on something that is very difficult for them. When we actively work to maintain and preserve our children's self-esteem, they will keep trying when tasks are difficult, even when they feel they are failing. The tips previously mentioned can help them persevere through the most challenging tasks, so when each task is over, they can relish that they worked through them. Over time, this is how your guidance can assist them develop stamina and strong work ethics.

LEARN HOW POWERFUL YOU CAN BE

You hear it all the time, "Successful readers read to their parents every night." TRANSLATION: "Non-dyslexic readers read to their parents every night." Many teachers and parents do not understand the difficulties and pain associated with students who struggle learning to read. Many get on their high horse, touting how important it is for *your* child to read to *you* every day. Those teachers and parents have no idea what we go through, the tears, the shame, the exasperation, over and over. It's no wonder we quit. We begin to think we're doing more harm than good by forcing our struggling reader to read.

The *real* problem is not dyslexia or ADHD or learning a new language. Rather, it's the feeling of powerlessness that parents and teachers feel. When our children struggle in school, we feel powerless. If parents and teachers only knew that *they do have* the most powerful effect on the academic success of their children. Indeed, it is the people closest who can help the most, hands down. Yet, parents and many teachers of struggling students feel powerless and everyone continues to struggle!

If that's not enough, society gives us built-in excuses that reinforce why we should give up... "Public schools are to blame," "We both work and there's just no time," and "I don't have the money for a tutor." We are using these damaging myths as excuses for not fixing the problem.

If your school is not able to provide the support your child needs, your parental or teacher involvement is critical. I created a simplified method to empower parents, tutors, and teachers who are not reading specialists. You can learn as your student learns. You can have an impact on your child's achievement in reading, spelling, and writing.

The real problem: Powerlessness.

The real solution: Understand and learn how powerful you can be.

Your homework: First, write down your goals for your child in the following chart. Next, write down the steps you can take towards making each goal happen. Then take action.

Figure 1.5 Actions Should Be Based on Goals

Goals	What You Can Do at School	What You Can Do at Home	Specific Actions You Will Take

Several years ago, my dyslexic sons were my first students. Working with them was like walking across a bridge to a place I'd never been before. Also, it was no longer possible to go back to the way it was, because the bridge I'd crossed had disappeared. I understood clearly that I was in new territory and I wanted to understand this new place. In the process, I began to understand my children's strengths and weaknesses so that I could healthily address their weaknesses and foster their strengths. As a result, our lives began to change. Before I crossed the bridge, I was frustrated and hostile when working with my sons. After crossing, I practiced patience. Before they were aware of the source of their challenges, they would call themselves stupid when experiencing difficulties related to their dyslexia. But after I explained to them that they had dyslexia, it was as if a burden had been lifted. Over time, they began to understand that their difficulties were not related to a lack of intelligence, and they came to see how smart they really are. It was then my sons started to understand why they had to work harder than everyone else, and subsequently they went through an academic growth spurt.

I want to end this unit by sharing my own experience having dyslexia. We, struggling students (whether from dyslexia, ADHD, learning English, autism, or orthographic processing difficulties) mistakenly feel like we are stuck on the bottom rungs of the ladder of success. And in spite of how hard we try, that feeling is reinforced with repeated failures. As if that's not enough, we are confronted by a mentality telling us that the bottom rungs are where we are meant to be. Dear reader, it has taken me years to learn *we all have the potential to move up (or down) that ladder of success.* As teachers and parents, we can actively help our struggling students to stop viewing themselves at the bottom rung of a stationary ladder. We can strive to cultivate a healthier mentality by providing instruction that builds skills whereby a student at the bottom of the class can escalate and rise above their current challenges.

Dear reader, every struggling student needs an inspiration, someone who cares, someone who will have patience, no matter what. If you need help in this area, you can refer to my other book, *Cultivating Respect and Cooperation in the Classroom and at Home* (2018).

Always practice patience and actively inspire your child up the rungs of the ladder. No matter what has prevented your child or student from being able to reach the next step up, you should always search to understand, to communicate positively, to healthily address their weaknesses, and to foster their strengths. And in doing so, lives will change, including your own.

STEP 1 | TEACH SHORT VOWELS AND THEIR SOUNDS

> *As I begin my journey, I know my destination. I have the end in sight, and I'll get there… Even though I must build my ship as I sail it.*
>
> Laurie Hunter
> *Journal 5-26-04*

CREATE A SCHEDULE

It will take about 5 weeks to complete Steps 1 through 8 if you work one hour a day, 5 days a week. During the school year, the recommended schedule is 3 times a week for one hour OR 5 times a week for 30 minutes. **No matter what schedule you choose, each unit is intended to be covered swiftly. Do not take longer than 12 weeks to complete Steps 1 through 7.** It is vital for the instructor to introduce all the phonic orthographic spelling patterns that makeup words in the English language within 3 months' time.

Also, the timeframes listed on each individual activity are estimates. The student should complete as many activities he or she can comfortably do each day.

DO NOT SKIP ANY OF THE LESSONS

This instruction manual is devoted to teaching parents, teachers, and tutors how to provide reading intervention to their children and students who struggle learning to read. As an instructor, you do not have to read this entire manual before working with your child or student. Study one unit at a time (in order) then begin working on the activities from the unit. Activities are in the order they are to be completed.

Do not skip any of the lessons for your student to achieve maximum results. Also, date each activity to monitor that you are swiftly working through each unit.

Steps 1 and 2 introduce single letters and their sounds, like c, a, o, and e in the words <u>c</u>at, <u>a</u>pple, <u>o</u>ctopus, and <u>e</u>gg. This unit directly and explicitly teaches the alphabet letters, along with their sounds, so that students build a strong relationship with each of the 26 letters and their sounds. Students practice identifying the first 26 sounds in words and are also introduced to *stringing the sounds together* (blending) to make words.

BEGIN WITH WORDS THAT HAVE LETTERS WHICH CONSISTENTLY REPRESENT THEIR SOUNDS

Research on early reading instruction has demonstrated repeatedly that students master decoding with a code-based approach. Instructors should teach beginner readers that letters make consistent speech sounds (Richards cites Lyon 1999, 21). For instance, words like *cat*, *pig*, and *sun* have letters that make sounds consistently and predictably. However, some examples of words with letters that do not represent their typical sounds are: *buy*, *could*, *some*, and *there*. Using too many words like these when a student is learning to read creates uncertainty and poor confidence in reading.

A new reader needs to know that he or she can count on words just as you can count on people. Think about it. When you trust that a person can reliably come through for you, you build trust. You have confidence in that person. If a person does not reliably come through for you, or rather is perceived as inconsistent, you will not trust that person, and you most likely will distance yourself, maybe even dislike that person. Similarly, a child's introduction to the world of words must involve a *majority* of words whereby the letters consistently represent their sounds in the English language. This helps new readers build trust and confidence in words and in their reading ability.

All students should begin this reading program by building a foundation and a relationship with the letters and their corresponding primary sounds, even students who "struggle with comprehension only." A student who is working too hard decoding words could have difficulty comprehending text. Every student will benefit from confirming their knowledge of the letters and their sounds.

STUDY THE SPEECH SOUNDS

There are 44 phonemes in the English language. Phonemes are the smallest sounds of speech. Readers transform written letters into sounds. A letter between slashes like /f/ represents the sound f makes in the word *fish*. It is composed of three phonemes /f/ /i/ /sh/.

Below are the first 26 sounds. Try to say the sound of the letter first, then listen for the sound in the word. Repeat this exercise until you are familiar with every sound. Did you notice the positioning of your tongue, jaw, and lips change with each sound? Can you think of another word that begins with each sound? The vowels are highlighted and have multiple sounds, be sure to think of words that match the sound in the keyword.

/a/ apple

/b/ bird

/c/ cat

/d/ donut

/e/ elephant

/f/ fish

/g/ gum

/h/ hand

/i/ igloo

/j/ jam

/k/ kite

/l/ lion

/m/ monkey

/n/ napkin

/o/ octopus

/p/ pig

/q/ quarter

/r/ rainbow

/s/ snake

/t/ tiger

/u/ umbrella

/v/ van

/w/ watch

/x/ x-ray, box

/y/ yo-yo

/z/ zebra

CULTIVATING READING AND PHONICS SKILLS 1ˢᵀ GRADE – 3ᴿᴰ GRADE

FAMILIARIZE YOURSELF WITH THE 3-D VISUAL AIDS

Younger students and English Language Learners will need 3-D visuals to make their own set of 3-D Flash Cards. Older students who are learning to read can look at images on the Internet to make their Flash Cards. Either way, you will introduce each letter with a corresponding keyword and 3-dimensional visual aid or image. Students create their own 3-D Flash cards by drawing a picture of the visual and linking the mental image and keyword to its corresponding letter and sound. For instance, the first 3-D Flash Card the student will make is for the letter *a*, which makes the /a/ sound. It is the first sound in the word *apple*. The student can link letter *a* and the /a/ sound with the image of an apple.

It is essential that your student makes the 3-D Flash Cards. This will help him or her anchor the letters with their sounds. Also, later this will become very valuable during your discussions with the student. When the student is working on sound confusions, you will be able to help them distinguish the differences between similar sounds, such as /e/ and /i/. For example, the word *pen* has the *elephant* sound, and the word *pin* has the *igloo* sound. /e/ and /i/ sound a lot alike, but they are not.

UNDERSTAND THE SIGNIFICANCE OF THE 3-D FLASH CARDS

On the 3-D Flash Cards, the students will draw a picture of the keyword for the sound. The student must draw the picture and not write any words on the cards.

It is extremely important to show the 3-D visual aid to the students as they create each 3-D Flash Cards. It is the first activity we do with the students. Each flash card will represent a sound of the English language. The student must see and feel the visual aid when they draw it on the 3-D Flash Card. This interaction is what makes the student's 3-D Flash Cards more meaningful than *any* manufactured flash card. The student's artistry and the visual image of an object that they have seen and touched, are entwined with pride in their creation.

When a new reader's eyes see the lines and curves of letters, it is difficult for the brain to recognize the tiniest parts of a word. That's why we introduce letters that look similar to each other. This way students may visually distinguish their differences from the beginning.

a e i o u – the short vowels

c s r n m x v w z – the short consonants

p q g y j – the consonants with tails

d l h b k t f – the tall consonants

As you work through each step, you will see how the student-created 3-D Flash Cards become more and more essential. One important reason is that the 3-D Flash Cards illustrate how the same letter can make different sounds.

For example, the letter y, as a consonant, makes the *yoyo* sound.

When it is on the end of a syllable, the letter y is a vowel that can make the *long e* sound in *baby* or the *long i* sound in *butterfly*.

When the y is not on the end of a syllable it can make the *short i* sound in *gym*.

Letters, letter groups, sounds, and phonic rules can be very confusing. Because the students create their 3-D Flash Cards themselves, and in a systematic and logical order, they will have much more success understanding and remembering it all. And you, as the instructor, can learn along with them!

MAKE 3-D FLASH CARDS FOR THE SHORT VOWEL SOUNDS (10 MINUTES)

MATERIALS – Visuals for each keyword; 3-D Flash Cards for the **Short Vowel Sounds** (See Appendix B); colored markers that include a **pink marker**

Short Vowel Sounds	Visual and Keyword
a	apple
e	elephant
i	igloo
o	octopus
u	umbrella

INSTRUCTOR SAYS – We're going to make a flash card for each of the short vowels in the table above. Each letter has a keyword that begins with a short vowel sound. For example, the keyword for the short vowel *a* is *apple*. What sound does *a* make in the word *apple*? /a/

As you make each card, color inside the outlined letter with the pink marker and practice saying the sound as you color it.

After you color in the vowels (*a e i o u*) with pink, I will show you a visual for each short vowel sound. You can use any color to draw the keyword and visual for each short vowel sound.

CULTIVATING READING AND PHONICS SKILLS 1ST GRADE – 3RD GRADE

We can link a visual image to each sound. For instance, the letter *e* is the *elephant* sound. The elephant is a visual image and keyword we assign to the sound. So, when sounds become confusing, we can say the keywords to distinguish the differences in similar sounds.

For example, the words *pen* and *pin* are often mispronounced. However, the word *pen* has the *elephant* sound, and the word *pin* has the *igloo* sound. The sounds for *e* and *i* are different. For instance, you wouldn't want to call your friend *Peg*, "*Pig*," would you?

NOTE for English language learners – If your student is learning English as a second language, be sure to provide a bridge that connects letters and sounds of the student's first language with corresponding letters and sounds they are learning in English. After your student makes each 3-D Flash Card, ask if there is a letter or letters that make the same sound in his or her language. If so, tell the student to write it on the back of the corresponding 3-D Flash Card.

3-D Flash Cards: **Short Vowel Sounds**
Student colors letters with a **pink marker** then draws the keyword for each letter.

CULTIVATING READING AND PHONICS SKILLS 1ST GRADE – 3RD GRADE

LISTEN FOR THE SHORT VOWEL SOUNDS (10 MINUTES)

NOTE – When you see a letter between slashes, do not say the name of the letter, instead **say the sound it makes**. Do not show the student how to spell the word. This is a listening exercise only. If the student confuses first and last, show them Appendix A.

INSTRUCTOR SAYS – In this activity you will listen for short vowel sounds in words.

The first sound you'll listen for is the *a*pple sound.

When I say the word *apple*, do you hear the /a/ sound in *apple*? It's the first sound, isn't it?

Where do you hear the /a/ sound in the word *cat*? Is it the first sound, the last sound, or in the middle? (middle)

Some sounds are harder to hear than others. If ever you can't hear a sound in a word:

1) Say the word out loud and listen for the sound again.

2) Then I'll say the sound and the word while you watch my mouth.

Where do you hear the /a/ sound in the word *astronaut*? First, last, or middle? (first)

land (middle)
add (first)
tractor (middle)

How many /a/ sounds do you hear in:

happy (one)
family (one)
camel (one)

Let's listen for the *e*lephant sound.

When I say the word *elephant*, do you hear the /e/ sound in *elephant*? It's the first sound, isn't it?

Where do you hear the /e/ sound in the word *desk*? First, last, or middle? (middle)

elbow (first)
best (middle)
web (middle)

How many /e/ sounds do you hear in:

yellow (one)
network (one)
pepper (one)

Let's listen for the *igloo* sound.

When I say the word *igloo*, do you hear the /i/ sound in *igloo*? It's the first sound, isn't it?

Where do you hear the /i/ sound in the word *dish*? First, last, or middle? (middle)

pig (middle)
ignore (first)
inchworm (first)
window (middle)

How many /i/ sounds do you hear in:

pillow (one)
inside (one)

Let's listen for the *octopus* sound.

When I say the word *octopus*, do you hear the /o/ sound in *octopus*? It's the first sound, isn't it?

Where do you hear the /o/ sound in the word *clock*? First, last, or middle? (middle)

ostrich (first)
frog (middle)
olive (first)

How many /o/ sounds do you hear in:

crossword (one)
soccer (one)
officer (one)

CULTIVATING READING AND PHONICS SKILLS 1ST GRADE – 3RD GRADE

Let's listen for the **u**mbrella sound.

When I say the word *umbrella*, do you hear the /u/ sound in *umbrella*? It's the first sound, isn't it?

Where do you hear the /u/ sound in the word *cup*? First, last, or middle? (middle)

under (first)
puppy (middle)
peanut (middle)

How many /u/ sounds do you hear in:

ladybug (one)
understand (one)
thunder (one)

WRITE THE SHORT VOWELS WHILE SAYING THEIR SOUNDS (10 MINUTES)

MATERIALS – **pink** pen, yellow marker, and the student's 3-D Flash Cards

NOTE – Students need practice in writing, just as much as reading. They can be better readers through these writing exercises. They complement each other.

Writing can be very difficult for some of the students. For those, we want to take a light-hearted approach. We want this to be fun. The students should use a **pink** colored pen or a thin marker to write with. Tell them they are artists and they are not just writing letters, but rather they are drawing them.

The student will write the sounds as well as decode (read) them. Handwriting is a multisensory activity a student can do to build a relationship with the letters and sounds through the motion of writing, seeing the symbol, and hearing the sound.

The student will learn that there are 3 main starting points for the 26 letters: the headline, the armline, and the footline. The motions from those starting points should be **consistently modeled and verbalized** by the instructor.

In the following activity, the **instructor models how to write a letter using a yellow marker** so that the student has to really look to decipher what and how they need to write. Then the student will trace over the instructor's yellow marker, saying the sound as it is written. Then ask the student to practice writing the letter independently. After a few attempts you may have to model writing the letter again with your yellow marker and ask the student to trace over it again. At the end of the exercise you will be able to tell which letters are most challenging for the student.

Consistently and gently reinforce how to properly write the letters. During the activity, draw a happy face above well-written letters to communicate instantly that the student is writing the letter correctly. This simple habit is encouraging, makes the student feel good, and results in more effective learning.

Throughout all the writing exercises, **it is most important to instruct the student to say the sound as it is written.** Also, tell the student to remember how it feels to write the sound. **With practice, the student will connect the sound, symbol, and motion.**

INSTRUCTOR SAYS – See the stick figure to the left of the margin.

See the stick figure on the left side of the page. He is going to be your guide who will help you learn how to write letters. Point to his head. See the line touching the guide's head. It is called the headline. Now point to his feet. The line touching his feet is called the footline. Point to his arms. See how his arms are between the headline and the footline.

(Richards, 1999, p 220)

headline
armline
footline

1) Find the letter **a** in the alphabet and circle it. What keyword did you draw for that letter? What sound does the letter make in the keyword?

2) I will write a dot with my yellow marker to show you where the starting point of the letter begins in relationship to the guide.

CULTIVATING READING AND PHONICS SKILLS 1ST GRADE – 3RD GRADE

The starting point is where we rest our marker to begin writing each letter. For the letter *a*, the starting point is the armline.

3) I'll model writing the letter **a**, "Start at the armline, go toward the guide, circle around to the footline and back up to the armline, then go down to the footline."

4) Trace over my yellow **a**, while you say the sound.

5) I'll write a yellow dot for you to independently draw the letter. (Say verbal cues while the student is writing).

Repeat 1 through 5 with letters **e i o** and then **u**.

Write the Short Vowels While Saying Their Sounds

a b c d e f g h i j k l m

n o p q r s t u v w x y z

a

e

i

o

u

CULTIVATING READING AND PHONICS SKILLS 1ST GRADE – 3RD GRADE

READ THE SHORT VOWELS (5 MINUTES)

INSTRUCTOR SAYS – Read the letters below from left to right and say each sound (Mercer & Campbell, 1997). Remember to say the short vowel sounds for a, e, i, o, u. If you make an error, I will say the correct sound.

NOTE – Make sure the student says the correct sound for every letter. It is helpful to say the keyword to yourself for the vowel sound you're listening for. So for example, when you see the letter *a*, say, "*apple*" to yourself as you listen for the *apple* sound. Short vowel keywords are: *apple, elephant, igloo, octopus, umbrella*.

If the student makes an error, say the correct sound. If the student makes more than three errors, ask the student to go over the exercise again. Praise the student for any self-corrections.

a	e	i	o	u
o	a	u	e	i
e	o	a	i	u
i	e	u	o	a
u	a	i	e	o
i	e	o	a	u

SPELL THE SHORT VOWELS (5 MINUTES)

MATERIALS – pink pen, yellow marker, and the student's 3-D Flash Cards

INSTRUCTOR SAYS – I will say the sounds from the exercise we just completed, and you will write the letter that makes that sound.

NOTE – Make sure the student writes the correct letter while saying the sound out loud. If the student misspells the letter, write the correct letter with the yellow marker while saying the sound. Ask the student to trace over your yellow marker. Then have them write it again independently while saying the sound.

If the student is having difficulty memorizing a sound or confusing it with another letter, get the student's 3-D Flash Card they are having difficulty learning and ask the student to glue pink pompoms over the letter on the card.

CULTIVATING READING AND PHONICS SKILLS 1ST GRADE – 3RD GRADE

Spell the Short Vowels

headline
armline
footline

a b c d e f g h i j k l m

n o p q r s t u v w x y z

STEP 2 | TEACH CONSONANTS AND THEIR SOUNDS

> *"A character that once seemed merely a lifeless and anonymous jumble of lines and dots becomes a 'character' in a different sense; that is, with a distinctive personality of its own."*
>
> Kenneth G. Henshall
> *A Guide to Remembering Japanese Characters*

MAKE 3-D FLASH CARDS FOR THE CONSONANT SOUNDS (30 MINUTES)

MATERIALS – Visuals for each keyword; 3-D Flash Cards for the **Consonant Sounds** (See Appendix B); colored markers that include a **green marker**

Consonant Sounds	Visual and Keyword
c	cat
s	snake
r	rainbow
n	napkin
m	monkey
x	x-ray, box
v	van
w	watch
z	zebra

INSTRUCTOR SAYS – The word *sun* has 3 letters. Watch me as I point to each sound as I read it.

CULTIVATING READING AND PHONICS SKILLS 1ST GRADE – 3RD GRADE

s   u   n

What is a consonant?

We learned that the letters a, e, i, o, and u are vowels. What are all the other letters called? All the other letters are called consonants. The letter y is the only letter that can be a vowel and a consonant.

As you make each flash card, I will ask you to listen for the sounds inside of words.

NOTE for English language learners – If your student is learning English as a second language, be sure to provide a bridge that connects letters and sounds of the student's first language with corresponding letters and sounds they are learning in English. After your student makes each 3-D Flash Card, ask if there is a letter or letters that make the same sound in his or her language. If so, tell the student to write it on the back of the corresponding 3-D Flash Card.

LISTEN FOR THE CONSONANT SOUNDS (20 MINUTES)

NOTE – When you see a letter between slashes, do not say the name of the letter, instead **say the sound it makes**. Do not show the student how to spell the word. This is a listening exercise only. If the student confuses first and last show them Appendix A.

INSTRUCTOR SAYS – In this activity you will listen for consonant sounds in words.

Take a look at the flash card for the letter **c**.
The keyword for the letter **c** is **c**at. What sound does **c** make in the word **c**at? /c/
Trace over the letter **c** and say the sound as you write it.
Here is a visual of the keyword for you to draw on your flash card.
Where do you hear the /c/ sound? Is it the first or the last sound you hear?

cow (first)
catch (first)
sock (last)
How many /c/ sounds do you hear in:
coconut (2)
clock (2)

Take a look at the flash card for the letter *s*.
The keyword for the letter *s* is *snake*. What sound does *s* make in the word *snake*? /s/
Trace over the letter *s* and say the sound as you write it.
Here is a visual of the keyword for you to draw on your flash card.
Where do you hear the /s/ sound? Is it the first sound or last sound you hear?

octopus (last)
spider (first)
How many /s/ sounds do you hear in:
sister (2)
sweater (1)

Take a look at the flash card for the letter *r*.
The keyword for the letter *r* is *rainbow*. What sound does *r* make in the word *rainbow*? /r/
Trace over the letter *r* and say the sound as you write it.
Here is a visual of the keyword for you to draw on your flash card.
Where do you hear the /r/ sound? Is it the first sound or last sound you hear?
ring (first)
bear (last)
How many /r/ sounds do you hear in:
rabbit (1)
cover (1)

Take a look at the flash card for the letter *n*.
The keyword for the letter *n* is *napkin*. What sound does *n* make in the word *napkin*? /n/
Trace over the letter *n* and say the sound as you write it.
Here is a visual of the keyword for you to draw on your flash card.
Where do you hear the /n/ sound? Is it the first sound or last sound you hear?
moon (last)
nose (first)
How many /n/ sounds do you hear in:
nine (2)
napkin (2)

Take a look at the flash card for the letter *m*.
The keyword for the letter *m* is *monkey*. What sound does *m* make in the word *monkey*? /m/
Trace over the letter *m* and say the sound as you write it.
Here is a visual of the keyword for you to draw on your flash card.
Where do you hear the /m/ sound? Is it the first sound or last sound you hear?
moon (first)
mop (first)
How many /m/ sounds do you hear in:

CULTIVATING READING AND PHONICS SKILLS 1ST GRADE – 3RD GRADE

mom (2)
mummy (2)

Take a look at the flash card for the letter **x**.
The keyword for the letter **x** is **x**ray. What sound does **x** make in the word **x**ray? /x/
The letter x also makes the /cks/ sound at the end of the word bo**x**.

Trace over the letter **x** and say the sound as you write it.
Here is a visual of the keyword for you to draw on your flash card.
Where do you hear the /x/ sound? Is it the first sound or last sound you hear?
fox (last)
exercise (first/middle - Both are correct. The student may hear /x/ as the first sound heard. But some may hear /e/ first and /cks/ after, so middle is also correct.)
How many /x/ sounds do you hear in:
ax (1)
box (1)

Take a look at the flash card for the letter **v**.
The keyword for the letter **v** is **v**an. What sound does **v** make in the word **v**an? /v/
Trace over the letter **v** and say the sound as you write it.
Here is a visual of the keyword for you to draw on your flash card.
Where do you hear the /v/ sound? Is it the first sound or last sound you hear?
violin (first)
live (last)
How many /v/ sounds do you hear in:
heavy (1)
evening (1)

Take a look at the flash card for the letter **w**.
The keyword for the letter **w** is **w**atch. What sound does **w** make in the word **w**atch? /w/
Trace over the letter **w** and say the sound as you write it.
Here is a visual of the keyword for you to draw on your flash card.
Where do you hear the /w/ sound? Is it the first sound or last sound you hear?
wig (first)
work (first)
How many /w/ sounds do you hear in:
waffle (1)
wiggle (1)

Take a look at the flash card for the letter **z**.
The keyword for the letter **z** is **z**ebra. What sound does **z** make in the word **z**ebra? /z/
Trace over the letter **z** and say the sound as you write it.
Here is a visual of the keyword for you to draw on your flash card.

Where do you hear the /z/ sound? Is it the first sound or last sound you hear?
zipper (first)
freeze (last)
How many /z/ sounds do you hear in:
zigzag (2)
puzzle (1)

CULTIVATING READING AND PHONICS SKILLS 1ST GRADE – 3RD GRADE

3-D Flash Cards: **Consonant Sounds**
Student colors letters with a **green marker** then draws the keyword for each letter.

3-D Flash Cards: **Consonant Sounds**
Student colors letters with a **green marker** then draws the keyword for each letter.

WRITE THE CONSONANTS WHILE SAYING THEIR SOUNDS (30 MINUTES)

MATERIALS – **green** pen, yellow marker, and the student's 3-D Flash Cards

NOTE – Students need practice in writing, just as much as reading. They can be better readers through these writing exercises, where reading and writing complement each other. Writing can be very difficult for some of the students. For those, we want to take a light-hearted approach. We want this to be fun. The students should use a **green** pen or thin pencil-shaped marker. Tell them they are artists and they are not just writing letters, but rather they are drawing them.

The student will write the sounds as well as decode (read) them. Handwriting is a multisensory activity a student can do to build a relationship with the letters and sounds through the motion of writing, seeing the symbol, and hearing the sound.

CULTIVATING READING AND PHONICS SKILLS 1ST GRADE – 3RD GRADE

The student will learn that there are three main starting points for the 26 letters, the headline, the armline, and the footline. The motions from those starting points should be consistently *modeled* by the instructor.

The instructor models how to write a letter using a yellow marker so that the student has to really look to decipher what and how they need to write. Throughout all the writing exercises, it is most important to instruct the student to say the *sound* as it is written. Tell the student to remember how it *feels* to write the sound.

Draw a happy face to communicate instantly that the student is writing the letter correctly. This simple habit is encouraging, makes the student feel good, and results in more effective learning.

Consistently, and gently, reinforce how to properly write the letters. Telling the student once is not enough. Also, you may have to place a dot with your pen to remind them where the starting point is. Over time the student will connect the sound, symbol, and motion.

LAURIE HUNTER

Write the Consonants While Saying Their Sounds

abcdefghijklm

nopqrstuvwxyz

c

s

r

n

m

(see back)

CULTIVATING READING AND PHONICS SKILLS 1ST GRADE – 3RD GRADE

READ THE CONSONANT SOUNDS (5 MINUTES)

NOTE – Make sure the student says the correct sound for every letter. It is helpful to review the keywords and practice doing this activity by yourself before you do this with your student.

If the student makes an error, say the correct sound immediately. If the student makes more than three errors, ask the student to go over the exercise again. *Praise* the student for any self-corrections.

INSTRUCTOR SAYS – Read the letters below from left to right and say each sound. If you make an error, I will say the correct sound.

c	s	r	n	m
x	v	w	z	s
n	x	w	c	r
m	v	z	r	x
z	s	m	w	c
n	w	m	c	x

CULTIVATING READING AND PHONICS SKILLS 1ST GRADE – 3RD GRADE

SPELL THE CONSONANT SOUNDS (5 MINUTES)

MATERIALS – green pen, yellow marker, and the student's 3-D Flash Cards

INSTRUCTOR SAYS – I will say the sounds from the exercise we just completed, and you will write the letter that makes that sound.

NOTE – Make sure the student writes the correct letter while saying the sound out loud. If the student misspells the letter, write the correct letter with the yellow marker while saying the sound. Ask the student to trace over your yellow marker. Then have them write it again independently while saying the sound.

If the student is having difficulty memorizing a sound or confusing it with another letter, get the student's 3-D Flash Card they are having difficulty learning and ask the student to glue green pompoms over the letter on the card.

Spell the Consonant Sounds

headline
armline
footline

abcdefghijklm

nopqrstuvwxyz

CULTIVATING READING AND PHONICS SKILLS 1ST GRADE – 3RD GRADE

MAKE 3-D FLASH CARDS FOR THE CONSONANT SOUNDS (30 MINUTES)

MATERIALS – Visuals for each keyword; 3-D Flash Cards for the **Consonant Sounds** (See Appendix B); colored markers that include a **green marker**

Consonant Sounds	Visual and Keyword
p	pig
q	quarter
g	gum
y	yo-yo
j	jar of jam

INSTRUCTOR SAYS – The word *pig* has 3 letters. Watch me as I read each letter one sound at a time.

p   i   g

What is a consonant?

We learned that the letters *a, e, i, o,* and *u* are vowels. What are all the other letters called? All the other letters are called consonants. The letter y is the only letter that can be a vowel and a consonant. When y makes the yoyo sound, it is a consonant sound. We will discuss later when the letter y is a vowel.

As you make each flash card, I will ask you to listen for the sounds inside of words.

NOTE for English language learners – If your student is learning English as a second language, be sure to provide a bridge that connects letters and sounds of the student's first language with corresponding letters and sounds they are learning in English. After your student makes each 3-D Flash Card, ask if there is a letter or letters that make the same sound in his or her language. If so, tell the student to write it on the back of the corresponding 3-D Flash Card.

LISTEN FOR THE CONSONANT SOUNDS (10 MINUTES)

NOTE – When you see a letter between slashes, do not say the name of the letter, instead **say the sound it makes**. Do not show the student how to spell the word. This is a listening exercise only. If the student confuses first and last show them Appendix A.

INSTRUCTOR SAYS – In this activity you will listen for consonant sounds in words.

Take a look at the flash card for the letter *p*.
The keyword for the letter *p* is *p*ig. What sound does *p* make in the word *p*ig? /p/
Trace over the letter *p* and say the sound as you write it.
Here is a visual of the keyword for you to draw on your flash card.
Where do you hear the /p/ sound? Is it the first sound or last sound you hear?
cup (last)
grape (last)
How many /p/ sounds do you hear in:
puppy (2)
purple (2)

Take a look at the flash card for the letter *q*.
The keyword for the letter *q* is *q*uarter. What sound does *q* make in the word *q*uarter? /q/
Trace over the letter *q* and say the sound as you write it.
Here is a visual of the keyword for you to draw on your flash card.
Where do you hear the /q/ sound? Is it the first sound or last sound you hear?
quiet (first)
quilt (first)
How many /q/ sounds do you hear in:
frequent (1)
queen (1)

Take a look at the flash card for the letter *g*.
The keyword for the letter *g* is *g*um. What sound does *g* make in the word *g*um? /g/
Trace over the letter *g* and say the sound as you write it.
Here is a visual of the keyword for you to draw on your flash card.
Where do you hear the /g/ sound? Is it the first sound or last sound you hear?
egg (last)
flag (last)
How many /g/ sounds do you hear in:
gorilla (1)
giggle (2)

CULTIVATING READING AND PHONICS SKILLS 1ST GRADE – 3RD GRADE

Take a look at the flash card for the letter **y**.
The keyword for the letter **y** is **y**o**y**o. What sound does **y** make in the word **y**o**y**o? /y/
Trace over the letter **y** and say the sound as you write it.
Here is a visual of the keyword for you to draw on your flash card.
Where do you hear the /y/ sound? Is it the first sound or last sound you hear?
yak (first)
young (first)
How many /y/ sounds do you hear in:
yoyo (2)
yummy (1)

Take a look at the flash card for the letter *j*.
The keyword for the letter *j* is *j*ar. What sound does *j* make in the word *j*ar and *j*am? /j/
Trace over the letter *j* and say the sound as you write it.
Here is a visual of the keyword for you to draw on your flash card.
Where do you hear the /j/ sound? Is it the first sound or last sound you hear?
jelly (first)
large (last)
How many /j/ sounds do you hear in:
jungle (1)
injury (1)

LAURIE HUNTER

3-D Flash Cards: **Consonant Sounds**
Student colors letters with a **green marker** then draws the keyword for each letter.

43

CULTIVATING READING AND PHONICS SKILLS 1ST GRADE – 3RD GRADE

WRITE THE CONSONANT SOUNDS (10 MINUTES)

MATERIALS – green pen, yellow marker, and the student's 3-D Flash Cards

NOTE – Students need practice in writing, just as much as reading. They can be better readers through these writing exercises, where reading and writing complement each other. Writing can be very difficult for some of the students. For those, we want to take a light-hearted approach. We want this to be fun. The students should use a green pen or thin pencil-shaped marker of their choice. Tell them they are artists and they are not just writing letters, but rather they are drawing them.

The student will write the sounds as well as decode (read) them. Handwriting is a multisensory activity a student can do to build a relationship with the letters and sounds through the motion of writing, seeing the symbol, and hearing the sound.

The student will learn that there are three main starting points for the 26 letters, the headline, the armline, and the footline. The motions from those starting points should be consistently *modeled* by the instructor.

The instructor models how to write a letter using a yellow marker, so that the student has to really look to decipher what and how they need to write. Throughout all the writing exercises it is most important to instruct the student to say the *sound* as it is written. Tell the student to remember how it *feels* to write the sound.

Draw a happy face to communicate instantly that the student is writing the letter correctly. This simple practice is encouraging, makes the lesson more enjoyable, and results in more effective learning.

Consistently, and gently, reinforce how to properly write the letters. Telling the student once is not enough. Also, you may have to place a dot with your pen to remind them where the starting point is. Over time the student will connect the sound, symbol, and motion.

Write the Consonants While Saying Their Sounds

CULTIVATING READING AND PHONICS SKILLS 1ST GRADE – 3RD GRADE

READ THE CONSONANT & VOWEL SOUNDS (5 MINUTES)

 **NOTE** – Make sure the student says the correct sound for every letter. It is helpful to review the keywords and practice doing this activity by yourself before you do this with your student.

If the student makes an error, say the correct sound immediately. If the student makes more than three errors, ask the student to go over the exercise again. *Praise* the student for any self-corrections.

 **INSTRUCTOR SAYS** – Read the letters below from left to right and say each sound. If you make an error, I will say the correct sound.

p	q	g	y	j
q	g	p	j	y
p	a	q	e	g
i	y	o	j	u
q	p	g	y	j
a	e	i	o	u

SPELL THE CONSONANT SOUNDS (5 MINUTES)

MATERIALS – green pen, yellow marker, and the student's 3-D Flash Cards

INSTRUCTOR SAYS – I will say the sounds from the exercise we just completed, and you will write the letter that makes that sound.

NOTE – Make sure the student writes the correct letter while saying the sound out loud. If the student misspells the letter, write the correct letter with the yellow marker while saying the sound. Ask the student to trace over your yellow marker. Then have them write it again independently while saying the sound.

If the student is having difficulty memorizing a sound or confusing it with another letter, get the student's 3-D Flash Card they are having difficulty learning and ask the student to glue green pompoms over the letter on the card.

CULTIVATING READING AND PHONICS SKILLS 1ST GRADE – 3RD GRADE

Spell the Consonant Sounds

abcdefghijklm
nopqrstuvwxyz

MAKE 3-D FLASH CARDS FOR THE CONSONANT SOUNDS (30 MINUTES)

MATERIALS – Visuals for each keyword; 3-D Flash Cards for the **Consonant Sounds** (See Appendix B); colored markers that include a **green marker**

Consonant Sounds	Visual and Keyword
d	donut
l	lion
h	hand
b	bird
k	kite
t	tiger
f	fish

INSTRUCTOR SAYS – The word *hot* has three letters. Watch me as I read each letter one sound at a time.

h   o   t

What is a consonant?
We learned that the letters *a, e, i, o,* and *u* are vowels. Remember, if a letter is not a vowel, then it is a consonant.

Take a look at the flash cards for the next set of consonants.
Notice how the letters d l h b k t f are all tall.

As you make each flash card, I will ask you to listen for the sounds inside of words.

NOTE for English language learners – If your student is learning English as a second language, be sure to provide a bridge that connects letters and sounds of the student's first language with corresponding letters and sounds they are learning in English. After your student makes each 3-D Flash Card, ask if there is a letter or letters that make the same sound in his or her language. If so, tell the student to write it on the back of the corresponding 3-D Flash Card.

CULTIVATING READING AND PHONICS SKILLS 1ST GRADE – 3RD GRADE

LISTEN FOR THE CONSONANT SOUNDS (20 MINUTES)

NOTE – When you see a letter between slashes, do not say the name of the letter, instead **say the sound it makes**. Do not show the student how to spell the word. This is a listening exercise only. If the student confuses first and last show them Appendix A.

INSTRUCTOR SAYS – In this activity you will listen for consonant sounds in words.

Take a look at the flash card for the letter *d*.
The keyword for the letter *d* is *d*onut. What sound does *d* make in the word *d*onut? /d/
Trace over the letter *d* and say the sound as you write it.
Here is a visual of the keyword for you to draw on your flash card.
Where do you hear the /d/ sound? Is it the first sound or last sound you hear?
dance (first)
read (last)
How many /d/ sounds do you hear in:
dad (2)
dinosaur (1)

Take a look at the flash card for the letter *l*.
The keyword for the letter *l* is *l*ion. What sound does *l* make in the word *l*ion? /l/
Trace over the letter *l* and say the sound as you write it.
Here is a visual of the keyword for you to draw on your flash card.
Where do you hear the /l/ sound? Is it the first sound or last sound you hear?
lap (first)
tall (last)
How many /l/ sounds do you hear in:
little (2)
lily (2)

Take a look at the flash card for the letter *h*.
The keyword for the letter *h* is *h*and. What sound does *h* make in the word *h*and? /h/
Trace over the letter *h* and say the sound as you write it.
Here is a visual of the keyword for you to draw on your flash card.
Where do you hear the /h/ sound? Is it the first sound or last sound you hear?
horse (first)
hop (first)
How many /h/ sounds do you hear in:
harmonica (1)
happy (1)

Take a look at the flash card for the letter *b*.
The keyword for the letter *b* is *bird*. What sound does *b* make in the word *bird*? /b/
Trace over the letter *b* and say the sound as you write it.
Here is a visual of the keyword for you to draw on your flash card.
Where do you hear the /b/ sound? Is it the first sound or last sound you hear?
ball (first)
grab (last)
How many /b/ sounds do you hear in:
bubble (2)
baby (2)

Take a look at the flash card for the letter *k*.
The keyword for the letter *k* is *kite*. What sound does *k* make in the word *kite*? /k/
Trace over the letter *k* and say the sound as you write it.
Here is a visual of the keyword for you to draw on your flash card.
Where do you hear the /k/ sound? Is it the first sound or last sound you hear?
book (last)
key (first)
How many /k/ sounds do you hear in:
monkey (1)
milkshake (2)

Take a look at the flash card for the letter *t*.
The keyword for the letter *t* is *tiger*. What sound does *t* make in the word *tiger*? /t/
Trace over the letter *t* and say the sound as you write it.
Here is a visual of the keyword for you to draw on your flash card.
Where do you hear the /t/ sound? Is it the first sound or last sound you hear?
dirt (last)
taste (first and last)
How many /t/ sounds do you hear in:
turtle (2)
teapot (2)

Take a look at the flash card for the letter *f*.
The keyword for the letter *f* is *fish*. What sound does *f* make in the word *fish*? /f/
Trace over the letter *f* and say the sound as you write it.
Here is a visual of the keyword for you to draw on your flash card.
Where do you hear the /f/ sound? Is it the first sound or last sound you hear?
frog (first)
cliff (last)
How many /f/ sounds do you hear in:
fluffy (2)
muffin (1)

CULTIVATING READING AND PHONICS SKILLS 1ST GRADE – 3RD GRADE

3-D Flash Cards: **Consonant Sounds**
Student colors letters with a **green marker** then draws the keyword for each letter.

3-D Flash Cards: **Consonant Sounds**
Student colors letters with a **green marker** then draws the keyword for each letter.

WRITE THE CONSONANT SOUNDS (20 MINUTES)

MATERIALS – **green** pen, yellow marker, and the student's 3-D Flash Cards

NOTE – Students need practice in writing, just as much as reading. They can be better readers through these writing exercises, where reading and writing complement each other. Writing can be very difficult for some of the students. For those, we want to take a light-hearted approach. We want this to be fun. The students should use a **green** pen or thin pencil-shaped marker of their choice. Tell them they are artists and they are not just writing letters, but rather they are drawing them.

The student will write the sounds as well as decode (read) them. Handwriting is a multisensory activity a student can do to build a relationship with the letters and sounds through the motion of writing, seeing the symbol, and hearing the sound.

CULTIVATING READING AND PHONICS SKILLS 1ST GRADE – 3RD GRADE

The student will learn that there are three main starting points for the 26 letters, the headline, the armline, and the footline. The motions from those starting points should be consistently *modeled* by the instructor.

The instructor models how to write a letter using a yellow marker so that the student has to really look to decipher what and how they need to write. Throughout all the writing exercises it is most important to instruct the student to say the *sound* as it is written. Tell the student to remember how it *feels* to write the sound.

Draw a happy face to communicate instantly that the student is writing the letter correctly. This simple practice is encouraging, makes the lesson more enjoyable, and results in more effective learning.

Consistently gently reinforce how to properly write the letters. Telling the student once is not enough. Also, you may have to place a dot with your pen to remind them where the starting point is. Over time the student will connect the sound, symbol, and motion.

Write the Consonants While Saying Their Sounds

CULTIVATING READING AND PHONICS SKILLS 1ST GRADE – 3RD GRADE

READ THE CONSONANT SOUNDS (5 MINUTES)

NOTE – Make sure the student says the correct sound for every letter. It is helpful to review the keywords and practice doing this activity by yourself before you do this with your student.

If the student makes an error, say the correct sound immediately. If the student makes more than three errors, ask the student to go over the exercise again. *Praise* the student for any self-corrections.

INSTRUCTOR SAYS – Read the letters below from left to right and say each sound. If you make an error, I will say the correct sound.

d	l	h	b	k
t	f	d	h	l
k	t	h	f	b
l	b	d	h	t
f	k	l	t	f
d	b	k	h	b

SPELL THE CONSONANT SOUNDS (5 MINUTES)

MATERIALS – green pen, yellow marker, and the student's 3-D Flash Cards

INSTRUCTOR SAYS – I will say the sounds from the exercise we just completed, and you will write the letter that makes that sound.

NOTE – Make sure the student writes the correct letter while saying the sound out loud. If the student misspells the letter, write the correct letter with the yellow marker while saying the sound. Ask the student to trace over your yellow marker. Then have them write it again independently while saying the sound.

If the student is having difficulty memorizing a sound or confusing it with another letter, get the student's 3-D Flash Card they are having difficulty learning and ask the student to glue green pompoms over the letter on the card.

CULTIVATING READING AND PHONICS SKILLS 1ST GRADE – 3RD GRADE

Spell the Consonant Sounds

headline
armline
footline

a b c d e f g h i j k l m

n o p q r s t u v w x y z

STEP 3 | PROVIDE PRACTICE BLENDING SOUNDS TO MAKE WORDS

> *Today he walked out the door a different boy from the one that had walked in 20 minutes ago. I observed his smile, use of humor, skipping on his way out, and how he clutched his book in his hands with such a sense of accomplishment.*
>
> Laurie Hunter
> *Journal 2-28-04*

PROVIDE PRACTICE BLENDING USING 3-D FLASH CARDS, DOT TIME, AND SPOTLIGHTING

Now that the student has been acquainted with all the letters of the alphabet and their corresponding primary sounds, he or she is ready to blend the sounds to make words.

When the student struggles with a word, allow plenty of time to figure it out on his or her own, unless the word does not follow a pattern.

Help your student decode words using the following three strategies: 3-D Flash Cards, Dot Time, and Spotlighting.

3-D FLASH CARDS

While reading the first ten stories, use the student's 3-D Flash Cards to spell words that he or she reads incorrectly, or does not know, in the following manner.

Point to the card and ask the student, "What's this sound?" (Student says, "/ch/.")

CULTIVATING READING AND PHONICS SKILLS 1ST GRADE – 3RD GRADE

Instructor lays down the next 3-D Flash Card and asks, "What's this sound?" (Student says, "/o/.")

Ask the student to touch each card and say each sound as it is sounded out. (Student says, "/ch/ /o/.")

"Blend the sounds and touch the sounds as you say them." (Student says, "/cho/.")

"What's this sound?" (Student says, "/p/.")

"What do you have so far?" (Student touches the cards and says, " /cho/.")

"Blend the sounds to say the word." **Ask the student to touch each card as each one is sounded out, especially if the student has difficulty blending the sounds together.** (Student touches the cards and says, "/cho/ /p/," recognizes the word, blends the sounds together to say, "/chop/."

60

Figure 3.1 3-D Flash Cards

Benefits to Using the 3-D Flash Cards to Decode Words

The student uses the picture on the 3-D Flash Card as a prompt to retrieve the sound.

The student exercises memory recall of the sounds. The instructor strings the sounds in words by adding only one sound at a time. Each time a new 3-D Flash Card is added, the student must recall what he or she has blended so far.

The student can touch each sound as it is said so sounds are pronounced sequentially.

Many students may know the sounds each letter makes, but have difficulty blending the sounds accurately. By providing these students with repeated practice blending sounds, whereby the student touches each sound as it is said, accuracy will improve over time.

DOT TIME

You can also use Dot Time to blend sounds.

Write the first letter *n* on a dot sticker.

Hold it up to the student and ask, "What sound does this letter make?" When the student says "/n/," place the dot on a piece of paper.

Write the next letter *a* on another dot.

Ask the student, "What is this sound?"
When the student successfully says "/a/," point to the worksheet and ask, "What do you have so far?" When the student says "/n/," place the *a* next to the *n*.
The instructor says, "Now say the sounds together?"

CULTIVATING READING AND PHONICS SKILLS 1ST GRADE – 3RD GRADE

Student will say "/na/."

Write the next letter *p* on another dot.

Ask the student, "What is this sound?"
When the student successfully says "/p/," point to the dots on the paper and ask, "What do you have so far?" When the student says "/na/," place the *p* next to the *a*.
The instructor says, "Now say the sounds together?"

Student will say "/nap/, nap."

Figure 3.2 Dot Time

> **Benefits to Using Dot Time to Decode Words**
>
> The student visually sees sound segmentation and how sounds blend to make words.
>
> Dot Time exercises memory recall of the sounds. The instructor strings the sounds in words by adding only one sound at a time. Each time a new dot (sound) is added, the student must recall what he or she has blended so far.
>
> This is multisensory learning that involves the student, which will more keenly engage the student's attention.

SPOTLIGHTING

Use Spotlighting when the student jumbles up the sequence of the sounds in a word. Use the Spotlight (penlight) to light up a word, sound by sound. The student is to say the sounds one at a time as you light them up. For example, if the student says "*snaps*" instead of *naps*, Spotlight the letter *n* to prompt the student to sound out the *n*. When successful, the instructor continues by Spotlighting the *a*. And so on.

Spotlighting is also effective when the student reads one sound in a word incorrectly. Use the Spotlight to light up the incorrect sound. For example, if student says, "*dug*" instead of *bug*, Spotlight the letter *b*, in the word bug to prompt the student to take a closer look at the *b*.

Figure 3.3 Spotlighting

Benefits of Spotlighting

Spotlighting aids the student in saying the sounds in sequential order.

Lighting letters as they are read helps the student map sounds to their corresponding letters (or letter group).

The light draws the instructor's and the student's attention to letters the student is repeatedly having difficulty with or is confusing with another letter. You'll begin to notice which letters the student is having the most difficulty remembering, because you'll have spotlighted those letters most often.

CULTIVATING READING AND PHONICS SKILLS 1ST GRADE – 3RD GRADE

INTRODUCE ROUND UP WORDS (5 MINUTES)

INSTRUCTOR SAYS – Some of the stories we are about to read may contain words that do not make the sounds you have learned yet. Other words you'll read may not follow a phonics pattern.

We'll "round up" those words by writing them down and reviewing them until we can recognize them by sight.

To "round up" a word I will write it with a yellow marker, and you will trace over the word. This ensures that the word will fit and be readable. Each day we'll review them until you commit them to memory.

NOTE – If the student already knows how to read a word that does not make the sounds we've studied so far, then there is no need to write that word down. For example, the student may already know that the *a* in the word *want* is not pronounced like the *a* in the keyword *apple*.

Also, later the student may figure out that a word on the Round Up paper does indeed follow a pattern after all. For example, in the first story the student may not recognize the word *by* and will write it down as a round up word. However, the student will learn later that the *y* can make the *long i* sound. When the student learns the spelling pattern of a word on the Round Up sheet, he or she can cross it out.

of	are
two	come
to	have
was	love
want	some
what	there
who	move
been	could
said	would
again	should
buy	
build	

Round Up Words

CULTIVATING READING AND PHONICS SKILLS 1ST GRADE – 3RD GRADE

READ THE STORIES (10 TO 30 MINUTES)

MATERIALS – "The Plan" found in *Phonics Stories: Short Vowels*, by Laurie Hunter; the student's 3-D Flash Cards; Dot Time stickers; Spotlighting finger lights

AT THE BEGINNING OF EVERY SESSION – Review the student's 3-D Flash Cards.

WHILE READING EACH STORY – Allow the student to practice blending difficult words using the 3-D Flash Cards, Dot Time, and/or Spotlighting.

EXPLAIN – While reading "The Plan," you might notice that the **th** letter group does not make the sounds you learned for **t** and **h**. You can add the word **the** to the Round Up paper, if you'd like. Also, you may not know the words **to** and **too** and can add them to the Round Up paper. We will learn the spelling patterns for these words later.

INSTRUCTOR SAYS – Read the story from the book, *Phonics Stories: Short Vowel Sounds*, while I follow along using this manual. If you don't know a word, or you make an error, I will spell the word with your 3-D Flash Cards or Dot Time stickers. When you use your flash cards or the stickers, always touch each letter as you say its sound. This will help strengthen your knowledge of the letters and their sounds.

NOTE – Place Dot Time stickers below for the student to practice difficult words.

The Plan

The cat is sad.
The cat is sad and mad.
Sam is a man.
The man, Sam, is sad and mad too.
The cat has a plan.
The cat's plan is to sit on Sam's lap
Sam is glad.
"I am glad I have a cat!"
Sam has a plan too.
Sam gets a can.
Sam gets a can of cat food.
The cat ran to Sam.
"I am glad I have Sam!"
The cat is glad to have Sam.

NOTE – If the student made three or more errors while reading the story, then have the student reread the story again to build word recognition and fluency. The student should reread and master each story before progressing to the next one.

SPELL WORDS FROM THE STORY (10 TO 30 MINUTES)

MATERIALS – Yellow marker and **pink** pen

INSTRUCTOR SAYS – Use the pink pen to circle the vowels (*a e i o u*) in the alphabet on the following page.

For this activity, I will select eight words from the story for you to spell. **The purpose of this exercise is for you to say each word you spell so slowly that you can hear each sound as you write each letter**.

Spelling Words from "The Plan"		
Short a sounds like **a**pple	Long a says its name	We'll learn the rules for these words later!
plan	a	the
cat		too
sad		to
and		I
mad		food
Sam		
man		
has		
cat's		
Sam's		
lap		
glad		
am		
have		
can		
ran		

CULTIVATING READING AND PHONICS SKILLS 1ST GRADE – 3RD GRADE

DURING THIS ACTIVITY – Cover the spelling words, so your student can't see them. Provide immediate feedback for correct responses with stars or happy faces. More importantly, provide immediate feedback for all errors by writing the correct word with a yellow marker and **ask the student to trace over each letter while saying its corresponding sound**.

EXPLAIN – Now look over all the words you spelled and circle with the pink pen the letter that makes short a sound, like in the word *apple*. Notice all the *a*'s you circled make a short a sound. When **a** is at the beginning or middle of a word, the **a** makes the *apple* sound. When **a** is on the end of a word, it can say its name. The word **a** makes the **long a** sound.

NOTE for English language learners – English language learners should sketch a drawing next to each word they spell, unless it is a word they already know. Talk about the meaning of each word. Afterwards, ask the student to create one sentence using two of the words. Model writing the sentence for the student with your yellow marker. Then ask the student to trace over your yellow marker.

Spell Short a Words While Saying Their Sounds

headline
armline
footline

a b c d e f g h i j k l m

n o p q r s t u v w x y z

CULTIVATING READING AND PHONICS SKILLS 1ST GRADE – 3RD GRADE

READ THE STORIES (10 TO 30 MINUTES)

 **MATERIALS** – "The Job" found in *Phonics Stories: Short Vowels*, by Laurie Hunter; the student's 3-D Flash Cards; Dot Time stickers; Spotlighting finger lights

AT THE BEGINNING OF EVERY SESSION – Review the student's 3-D Flash Cards.

WHILE READING EACH STORY – Allow the student to practice blending difficult words using the 3-D Flash Cards, Dot Time, and/or Spotlighting.

 **EXPLAIN** – While reading "The Job," you might notice that the **th** letter group does not make the sounds you learned for **t** and **h**. If not, let's add the words **the** and **with** on the Round Up paper. Also, you may not know the words **away**, **was**, **to, of**, and **saw** and can add them to the Round Up paper. We will learn the spelling patterns for these words later.

 **INSTRUCTOR SAYS** – Read the story from the book, *Phonics Stories: Short Vowel Sounds*, while I follow along using this manual. If you don't know a word, or you make an error, I will spell the word with your 3-D Flash Cards or Dot Time stickers. When you use your flash cards or the stickers, always touch each letter as you say its sound. This will help strengthen your knowledge of the letters and their sounds.

 **NOTE** – Place Dot Time stickers below for the student to practice difficult words.

The Job

I have a job.
I have a job, and my mom is the boss.
My job is to jog with the dog.
I jog with the dog a lot.

The dog ran off.
"Stop, Dog!"
Is he gone? Is he lost?

He is not gone.
The dog is on the hill,
He is not lost! I still have a job!

NOTE – If the student made three or more errors while reading the story, then have the student reread the story again to build word recognition and fluency. The student should reread and master each story before progressing to the next one.

SPELL WORDS FROM THE STORY (10 TO 30 MINUTES)

MATERIALS – Yellow marker and **pink** pen

INSTRUCTOR SAYS – Use the pink pen to circle the vowels (*a e i o u*) in the alphabet on the following page.

For this activity, I will select eight words from the story for you to spell. **The purpose of this exercise is for you to say each word you spell so slowly that you can hear each sound as you write each letter**.

Spelling Words for "The Job"	
Short o sounds like **o**ctopus	We'll learn the rules for these words later!
job	the
mom	I
boss	my
jog	to
dog	with
a lot	he
off	
stop	
gone	
lost	
not	
on	

DURING THIS ACTIVITY – Cover the spelling words, so student can't see them. Provide immediate feedback for correct responses with stars or happy faces. More importantly, provide immediate feedback for all errors by writing the correct word with a yellow marker and **ask the student to trace over each letter while saying its corresponding sound**.

CULTIVATING READING AND PHONICS SKILLS 1ST GRADE – 3RD GRADE

EXPLAIN – Now look over all the words you spelled and circle with the **pink** pen the letter that makes *short o* sound, like in the word *octopus*. Notice all the **o**'s you circled make a *short o* sound. When **o** is at the beginning or middle of a word, the **o** makes the **o***ctopus* sound. When **o** is on the end of a word, it can say its name. The word *n***o** makes the **long o** sound.

NOTE for English language learners – English language learners should sketch a drawing next to each word they spell, unless it is a word they already know. Talk about the meaning of each word. Afterwards, ask the student to create one sentence using two of the words. Model writing the sentence for the student with your yellow marker. Then ask the student to trace over your yellow marker.

Spell Short o Words While Saying Their Sounds

headline
armline
footline

abcdefghijklm
nopqrstuvwxyz

CULTIVATING READING AND PHONICS SKILLS 1ST GRADE – 3RD GRADE

READ THE STORIES (10 TO 30 MINUTES)

 **MATERIALS** – "Stuck!" found in *Phonics Stories: Short Vowels,* by Laurie Hunter; the student's 3-D Flash Cards; Dot Time stickers; Spotlighting finger lights

AT THE BEGINNING OF EVERY SESSION – Review the student's 3-D Flash Cards.

WHILE READING EACH STORY – Allow the student to practice blending difficult words using the 3-D Flash Cards, Dot Time, and/or Spotlighting.

 **EXPLAIN** – While reading "Stuck!" you might notice that the **th** letter group does not make the sounds you learned for *t* and *h*. If not, let's add the words **the**, **with**, **both**, and **this** on the Round Up paper. Also, you may not know the words **to**, **be**, and **now** and can add them to the Round Up paper. We will learn the spelling patterns for these words later.

 **INSTRUCTOR SAYS** – Read the story from the book, *Phonics Stories: Short Vowel Sounds,* while I follow along using this manual. If you don't know a word or make an error, I will spell the word with your 3-D Flash Cards or Dot Time stickers. When you use your flash cards or the stickers, always touch each letter as you say its sound. This will help strengthen your knowledge of the letters and their sounds.

 **NOTE** – Place Dot Time stickers below for the student to practice difficult words.

Stuck!

I tug. I tug, and I tug.
I huff, and I puff! I am stuck.
I am stuck in gum. It is not fun!
"Hum?"

I rub the gum.
I rub the gum to get it off.
The gum is stuck on my hands!
No luck! The gum is still stuck.
"Mom, help!"

Rub a dub dub!
I am in the tub.
Mom got the gum off with suds!

NOTE – If the student made three or more errors while reading the story, then have the student reread the story again to build word recognition and fluency. The student should reread and master each story before progressing to the next one.

SPELL WORDS FROM THE STORY (10 TO 30 MINUTES)

MATERIALS – Yellow marker and **pink** pen

INSTRUCTOR SAYS – Use the pink pen to circle the vowels (*a e i o u*) in the alphabet on the following page.

For this activity, I will select eight words from the story for you to spell. **The purpose of this exercise is for you to say each word you spell so slowly that you can hear each sound as you write each letter**.

Spelling Words for "Stuck!"	
Short u Sounds like **u**mbrella	We'll learn the rules for these words later!
stuck	I
tug	the
huff	my
puff	no
gum	with
fun	
hum	
rub	
luck	
dub dub	
tub	
suds	

CULTIVATING READING AND PHONICS SKILLS 1ST GRADE – 3RD GRADE

DURING THIS ACTIVITY – Cover the spelling words, so your student can't see them. Provide immediate feedback for correct responses with stars or happy faces. More importantly, provide immediate feedback for all errors by writing the correct word with a yellow marker and **ask the student to trace over each letter while saying its corresponding sound**.

EXPLAIN – Now look over all the words you spelled and circle with the pink pen the letter that makes *short u* sound, like in the word *umbrella*. Notice all the *u*'s you circled make a *short u* sound. When *u* is at the beginning or middle of a word, the *u* makes the *umbrella* sound. When *u* is on the end of a word, it can say its name. The letter *u* at the end of the word y*ou* makes the **long u** sound.

NOTE for English language learners – English language learners should sketch a drawing next to each word they spell, unless it is a word they already know. Talk about the meaning of each word. Afterwards, ask the student to create one sentence using two of the words. Model writing the sentence for the student with your yellow marker. Then ask the student to trace over your yellow marker.

Spell Short u Words While Saying Their Sounds

headline
armline
footline

abcdefghijklm
nopqrstuvwxyz

READ THE STORIES (10 TO 30 MINUTES)

MATERIALS – "My Twin Brother" found in *Phonics Stories: Short Vowels*, by Laurie Hunter; the student's 3-D Flash Cards; Dot Time stickers; Spotlighting finger lights

AT THE BEGINNING OF EVERY SESSION – Review the student's 3-D Flash Cards.

WHILE READING EACH STORY – Allow the student to practice blending difficult words using the 3-D Flash Cards, Dot Time, and/or Spotlighting.

EXPLAIN – While reading "My Twin Brother" you might notice that the **th** letter group does not make the sounds you learned for *t* and *h*. If not, let's add the words **the** and **brother** on the Round Up paper. Also, you may not know the words **my**, **to**, **because**, and **friend** and can add them to the Round Up paper. We will learn the spelling patterns for these words later.

INSTRUCTOR SAYS – Read the story from the book, *Phonics Stories: Short Vowel Sounds*, while I follow along using this manual. If you don't know a word, or you make an error, I will spell the word with your 3-D Flash Cards or Dot Time stickers. When you use your flash cards or the stickers, always touch each letter as you say its sound. This will help strengthen your knowledge of the letters and their sounds.

NOTE – Place Dot Time stickers below for the student to practice difficult words.

My Twin Brother

It spins and spins.
I miss. I miss six times.
"WIN BIG!"

It spins and spins.
I hit it six times. I win!
I win a big pig. But I am sick.

I sip water and sit still.
I am not sick.

I give the big pig to Nick.
Nick is my twin brother.
Nick is my twin brother and best friend.

 **NOTE** – If the student made three or more errors while reading the story, then have the student reread the story again to build word recognition and fluency. The student should reread and master each story before progressing to the next one.

SPELL WORDS FROM THE STORY (10 TO 30 MINUTES)

 **MATERIALS** – Yellow marker and pink pen

 **INSTRUCTOR SAYS** – Use the pink pen to circle the vowels (a e i o u) in the alphabet on the following page.

For this activity, I will select eight words from the story for you to spell. **The purpose of this exercise is for you to say each word you spell so slowly that you can hear each sound as you write each letter**.

Spelling Words for "My Twin Brother"		
Short i sounds like **i**gloo	Long i says its name	We'll learn the rules for these words later!
twin	I	my
it	times	brother
spins		water
miss		to
six		friend
hit		
win		
big		
pig		
sick		
sip		
sit		
still		
give		
Nick		
is		

CULTIVATING READING AND PHONICS SKILLS 1ST GRADE – 3RD GRADE

DURING THIS ACTIVITY – Cover the spelling words, so your student can't see them. Provide immediate feedback for correct responses with stars or happy faces. More importantly, provide immediate feedback for all errors by writing the correct word with a yellow marker and **ask the student to trace over each letter while saying its corresponding sound**.

EXPLAIN – Now look over all the words you spelled and circle with the **pink** pen the letter that makes *short i* sound, like in the word *igloo*. Notice all the *i*'s you circled make a *short i* sound. When *i* is at the beginning or middle of a word, the *i* makes the *igloo* sound. When *i* is on the end of a word, it can say its name. The words *I* and *hi* make the **long i** sound.

NOTE for English language learners – English language learners should sketch a drawing next to each word they spell, unless it is a word they already know. Talk about the meaning of each word. Afterwards, ask the student to create one sentence using two of the words. Model writing the sentence for the student with your yellow marker. Then ask the student to trace over your yellow marker.

Spell Short i Words While Saying Their Sounds

headline
armline
footline

abcdefghijklm

nopqrstuvwxyz

CULTIVATING READING AND PHONICS SKILLS 1ST GRADE – 3RD GRADE

READ THE STORIES (10 TO 30 MINUTES)

MATERIALS – "Like a Jet!" found in *Phonics Stories: Short Vowels*, by Laurie Hunter; the student's 3-D Flash Cards; Dot Time stickers; Spotlighting finger lights

AT THE BEGINNING OF EVERY SESSION – Review the student's 3-D Flash Cards.

WHILE READING EACH STORY – Allow the student to practice blending difficult words using the 3-D Flash Cards, Dot Time, and/or Spotlighting.

EXPLAIN – While reading "Like a Jet!" you might notice that the *i* in the word **like** does not make the short vowel sound you learned for *i*. If you haven't learned the word **like** yet, let's add it on the Round Up paper. Also, you may not know the words **ready, was, pain, wanted, race**, and **now** and can add them to the Round Up paper. We will learn the spelling patterns for these words later.

INSTRUCTOR SAYS – Read the story from the book, *Phonics Stories: Short Vowel Sounds*, while I follow along using this manual. If you don't know a word, or you make an error, I will spell the word with your 3-D Flash Cards or Dot Time stickers. When you use your flash cards or the stickers, always touch each letter as you say its sound. This will help strengthen your knowledge of the letters and their sounds.

NOTE – Place Dot Time stickers below for the student to practice difficult words.

Fast As a Jet!

Ready, set, go!
The bell went off!
Ed ran fast.
He ran fast as a jet
Ed was hot and getting red.
He fell.

He fell, but he got up and kept running.
He felt pain in his legs.
He wanted to yell.
He felt pain, but Ed kept running.
Ed saw the end of the race.
He did his best.
He did his best and wins the race.
Yes! Now, Ed can rest!

 **NOTE** – If the student made three or more errors while reading the story, then have the student reread the story again to build word recognition and fluency. The student should reread and master each story before progressing to the next one.

SPELL WORDS FROM THE STORY (10 TO 30 MINUTES)

 **MATERIALS** – Yellow marker and pink pen

 **INSTRUCTOR SAYS** – Use the pink pen to circle the vowels (*a e i o u*) in the alphabet on the following page.

For this activity, I will select eight words from the story for you to spell. **The purpose of this exercise is for you to say each word you spell so slowly that you can hear each sound as you write each letter.**

Spelling Words for "Like a Jet!"		
Short e sounds like elephant	Long e says its name	We'll learn the rules for these words later!
jet	the	ready
set	he	go
bell		was
went		pain
Ed		wanted
getting		to
red		saw
fell		race
kept		now
felt		
legs		
yell		
end		
best		
yes		
rest		

CULTIVATING READING AND PHONICS SKILLS 1ST GRADE – 3RD GRADE

DURING THIS ACTIVITY – Cover the spelling words, so your student can't see them. Provide immediate feedback for correct responses with stars or happy faces. More importantly, provide immediate feedback for all errors by writing the correct word with a yellow marker and **ask the student to trace over each letter while saying its corresponding sound**.

EXPLAIN – Now look over all the words you spelled and circle with the pink pen the letter that makes *short e* sound, like in the word *elephant*. Notice all the **e**'s you circled make a *short e* sound. When **e** is at the beginning or middle of a word, the **e** makes the *elephant* sound. When **e** is on the end of a word, it can say its name. The words h**e**, sh**e**, and w**e** make the **long e** sound.

NOTE for English language learners – English language learners should sketch a drawing next to each word they spell, unless it is a word they already know. Talk about the meaning of each word. Afterwards, ask the student to create one sentence using two of the words. Model writing the sentence for the student with your yellow marker. Then ask the student to trace over your yellow marker.

Spell Short e Words While Saying Their Sounds

headline
armline
footline

abcdefghijklm
nopqrstuvwxyz

CULTIVATING READING AND PHONICS SKILLS 1ST GRADE – 3RD GRADE

MAKE 3-D FLASH CARDS FOR THE CONSONANT SOUNDS (20 MINUTES)

MATERIALS – Visuals for the keywords; 3-D Flash Cards for the **Consonant Sounds** (See Appendix B); colored markers that include a **green marker**

Consonant Blends	Visual and Keyword
ch	chicken
sh	shell
th	three
ck	duck
wh	whale

INSTRUCTOR SAYS – The word *thick* has 5 letters, but only 3 sounds. Watch me as I point to each sound as I read it.

th   i   ck

What is a consonant? We learned that the letters *a, e, i, o,* and *u* are vowels. What are all the other letters called? All the other letters are called consonants. The letter *y* is the only letter that can be a vowel and a consonant.

Let's make flash cards for the consonants – ch sh th ck.
Take a look at the flash card for the letter *ch*.
The keyword for the letter *ch* is *chicken* What sound does *ch* make in the word *chicken*? /ch/
Trace over the letter *ch* and say the sound as you write it.
Here is a visual of the keyword for you to draw on your flash card.
Where do you hear the /ch/ sound? Is it the first sound or last sound?
peach (last)
chin (first)
How many /ch/ sounds do you hear?
inchworm (1)

Take a look at the flash card for the letter *sh*.
The keyword for the letter *sh* is *shell*. What sound does *sh* make in the word *shell*? /sh/
Trace over the letter *sh* and say the sound as you write it.

Here is a visual of the keyword for you to draw on your flash card.

Where do you hear the /sh/ sound? Is it the first sound or last sound?
crash (last)
shark (first)
How many /sh/ sounds do you hear?
trashcan (1)

Take a look at the flash card for the letter *th*.
The keyword for the letter *th* is *th*ree. What sound does *th* make in the word *th*ree? /th/
Trace over the letter *th* and say the sound as you write it.
Here is a visual of the keyword for you to draw on your flash card.
Where do you hear the /th/ sound? Is it the first sound or last sound?
think (first)
path (last)
How many /th/ sounds do you hear?
bathroom (1)

Take a look at the flash card for the letter *ck*.
The keyword for the letter *ck* is du*ck*. What sound does *ck* make in the word du*ck*? /ck/
Trace over the letter *ck* and say the sound as you write it.
Here is a visual of the keyword for you to draw on your flash card.
Where do you hear the /ck/ sound? Is it the first sound or last sound?
back (last)
sock (last)
How many /ck/ sounds do you hear?
locket (1)

NOTE for English language learners – If your student is learning English as a second language, be sure to provide a bridge that connects letters and sounds of the student's first language with corresponding letters and sounds they are learning in English. After your student makes each 3-D Flash Card, ask if there is a letter(s) that makes the same sound in his or her language. If so, tell the student to write it on the back of the corresponding 3-D Flash Card.

CULTIVATING READING AND PHONICS SKILLS 1ST GRADE – 3RD GRADE

3-D Flash Cards: **Consonant Sounds**
Student colors letters with a **green marker** then draws the keyword for each letter.

READ THE STORIES (10 TO 30 MINUTES)

MATERIALS – "The Chicken's Wish" found in Phonics Stories: Short Vowels, by Laurie Hunter; the student's 3-D Flash Cards; Dot Time stickers; Spotlighting penlight

AT THE BEGINNING OF EVERY SESSION – Review the student's 3-D Flash Cards.

WHILE READING EACH STORY – Allow the student to practice blending difficult words using the 3-D Flash Cards, Dot Time, and Spotlighting.

EXPLAIN – We noticed a few stories ago that the letters *t* and *h* in the word *the* do not make the *tiger* and *hand* sounds. When *t* and *h* are next to each other in words, together they make a whole new sound. It is a letter group, and we see **th** in words like *the* and the keyword *three*. The letters **ch** combine to make a whole new sound, and it's the first sound we hear in the keyword *chicken*. The same is true for letters **sh**, and it makes the first sound we hear in the word *she*.

INSTRUCTOR SAYS – Read the story from the book, *Phonics Stories: Short Vowel Sounds*, while I follow along using this manual. If you don't know a word, or you make an error, I will spell the word with your 3-D Flash Cards or Dot Time stickers. When you use your flash cards or the stickers, always touch each letter as you say its sound. This will help strengthen your knowledge of the letters and their sounds.

NOTE – Place Dot Time stickers below for the student to practice difficult words.

The Chicken's Wish

A chicken made a wish.
The chicken did not have much.
"I wish I was rich!"

"I think I will wish for a lot of cash."
She sat. She sat and waited.
She did not get rich. No luck!

She went back to the wishing well.
"What the heck!
I made a wish for cash so I can be rich.
But still no luck!"

The fish said to the chicken,
"More cash! I am going to be rich!
Thank you!

CULTIVATING READING AND PHONICS SKILLS 1ST GRADE – 3RD GRADE

NOTE – If the student made three or more errors while reading the story, then have the student reread the story again to build word recognition and fluency. The student should reread and master each story before progressing to the next one.

SPELL WORDS FROM THE STORY (10 TO 30 MINUTES)

MATERIALS – yellow marker and a **green** pen

INSTRUCTOR SAYS – Use the green marker to write the letter groups **wh th sh ch ck** above the alphabet.

For this activity I will ask you to spell words. You may know how to spell the words, but **the purpose of this exercise is for you say the word so slowly that you can hear all the sounds in each word and write each sound as you hear it**. Notice how all the words will follow patterns.

Spelling Words from "The Chicken's Wish"				
wh	**th**	**sh**	**ch**	**ck**
what	the	wish	chicken	chicken
	think	wishing	much	luck
	thank	cash	rich	back
		she		heck
		fish		

DURING THIS ACTIVITY – Cover the spelling words, so your student can't see them. Provide immediate feedback for correct responses with stars or happy faces. More importantly, provide immediate feedback for all errors by writing the correct word with a yellow marker and **ask the student to trace over each letter while saying its corresponding sound**.

EXPLAIN – Now look over all the words you spelled and circle with the **green** pen the letter groups **wh th sh ch ck**.

NOTE for English language learners – English language learners should sketch a drawing next to each word they spell, unless it is a word they already know. Talk about the meaning of each word. Afterwards, ask the student to create one sentence using two of the words. Model writing the sentence for the student with your yellow marker. Then ask the student to trace over your yellow marker.

Spell Short Vowel Words While Saying Their Sounds

headline
armline
footline

abcdefghijklm

nopqrstuvwxyz

CULTIVATING READING AND PHONICS SKILLS 1ST GRADE – 3RD GRADE

READ THE STORIES (10 TO 30 MINUTES)

MATERIALS – "Can You?" found in *Phonics Stories: Short Vowels*, by Laurie Hunter; the student's 3-D Flash Cards; Dot Time stickers; Spotlighting finger lights

AT THE BEGINNING OF EVERY SESSION – Review the student's 3-D Flash Cards.

WHILE READING EACH STORY – Allow the student to practice blending difficult words using the 3-D Flash Cards, Dot Time, and/or Spotlighting.

INSTRUCTOR SAYS – Read the story from the book, *Phonics Stories: Short Vowel Sounds*, while I follow along using this manual. If you don't know a word, or you make an error, I will spell the word with your 3-D Flash Cards or Dot Time stickers. When you use your flash cards or the stickers, always touch each letter as you say its sound. This will help strengthen your knowledge of the letters and their sounds.

NOTE – Place Dot Time stickers below for the student to practice difficult words.

Think About It

The chicken made a wish at the wishing well.
Did she have bad luck?
Can you get rich with a wish?

Nick and his twin brother are best friends.
He gave him a gift, a big pig.
Who is your best friend?

The dog ran off, and the girl was sad.
But the dog was not lost.
Have you lost a pet?

Sometimes we get stuck in gum.
Sometimes we get mad and sad.
Can you help someone that is mad or sad?

And Ed ran as fast as a jet.
He fell but kept running.
He did his best.
When you feel bad, can you still do your best?

SPELL WORDS FROM THE STORY (10 TO 30 MINUTES)

MATERIALS – Yellow marker and pink pen

INSTRUCTOR SAYS – Use the pink pen to circle the vowels (*a e i o u*) in the alphabet on the following page.

For this activity, I will select eight words from the story for you to spell. **The purpose of this exercise is for you to say each word you spell so slowly that you can hear each sound as you write each letter**.

Spelling Words from "Think About It"				
Short a sounds like apple	Short e sounds like elephant	Short i sounds like igloo	Short o sounds like octopus	Short u sounds like umbrella
at	well	think	dog	luck
have	get	it	off	but
bad	best	chicken	not	stuck
can	friends	wish	lost	gum
and	pet	wishing		running
ran	help	did		
sad	Ed	rich		
mad	jet	with		
that	fell	Nick		
fast	kept	his		
as	when	twin		
		him		
		gift		
		big		
		pig		
		is		
		in		
		still		

DURING THIS ACTIVITY – Cover the spelling words, so your student can't see them. Provide immediate feedback for correct responses with stars or happy faces. More importantly,

CULTIVATING READING AND PHONICS SKILLS 1ST GRADE – 3RD GRADE

provide immediate feedback for all errors by writing the correct word with a yellow marker and **ask the student to trace over each letter while saying its corresponding sound**.

EXPLAIN – Now look over all the words you spelled and circle with the **pink** pen the letter that makes *short vowel* sounds. Notice all the *short vowel* sounds you circled are at the beginning or middle of words, When **e** is on the end of a word, it can say its name. The words h**e**, sh**e**, and w**e** make the **long e** sound. But in the word **have** the **e** at the end of that word is **silent**.

NOTE for English language learners – English language learners should sketch a drawing next to each word they spell, unless it is a word they already know. Talk about the meaning of each word. Afterwards, ask the student to create one sentence using two of the words. Model writing the sentence for the student with your yellow marker. Then ask the student to trace over your yellow marker.

Spell Short Vowel Words Review

headline
armline
footline

a b c d e f g h i j k l m

n o p q r s t u v w x y z

CULTIVATING READING AND PHONICS SKILLS 1ST GRADE – 3RD GRADE

STEP 4 | TEACH LONG VOWELS AND THEIR SOUNDS

> *" I am not a product of my circumstances. I am a product of my decisions."*
>
> Stephen Covey

MAKE 3-D FLASH CARDS FOR VOWELS ON THE ENDS OF WORDS AND SYLLABLES (10 MINUTES)

MATERIALS – There are no visuals; 3-D Flash Cards for **Long Vowel Sounds: Vowels on the End of Words and Syllables** (See Appendix B); colored markers that include a **blue marker**

Long Vowel Sounds on the End of Words and Syllables	Keywords
a	a, cra-zy
e	me, me-te-or
i	I, ti-ger
o	no, pho-to
u	mu-sic, men-u

INSTRUCTOR SAYS – What are the vowels? (**a, e, i, o, u**, and sometimes **y**). The letter **y** is a consonant when it makes the **yoyo** sound. If the letter **y** is not making the **yoyo** sound, then it is a vowel.

Did you know that every word must have a vowel? Also, there must be a vowel in every syllable.

Vowels can make different sounds. There are short vowel sounds and long vowel sounds.

We learned the short vowel sounds first. Short vowels make the **a**pple, **e**lephant, **i**gloo, **o**ctopus, and **u**mbrella sounds.

Look at each Long Vowel Sounds 3-D Flash Card. It looks like the letter **a** is saying, "**a**." Trace over each long vowel with a blue marker. Say each long vowel sound as you write it. Trace over each long vowel (a, e, i, o, u) with blue marker and say its name.

What are the long vowel sounds? To hear long vowel sounds, just say the names of each of these vowels:

a   e   i   o   u

A long vowel sound is the name of a vowel.

There are different ways we can spell *long a*, *e*, *i*, *o*, and *u* sounds in the English language. One way to spell a long vowel sound is when **a vowel is on the end of a word the vowel can say its name**. One exception is the **silent e** and we'll talk about that soon.

Read the blue words below. Listen for the long vowel sounds on the end of each word:

b**e**   w**e**   h**e**   sh**e**   th**e**

Do you hear the *e* say, "e" in the words *be, we, he, she,* and *the*?

I   h**i**

Do you hear the *i* say, "i" in the words *I* and *hi*?

s**o**   n**o**   g**o**

Do you hear the *o* say, "o" in the words *so, no,* and *go*?

Long a, e, i, and o have only one sound, but long u has two sounds. What long vowel sound do you hear at the end of the word *menu*? Point to each sound as you say it.

men-**u**

Long u can also sound like "oo" at the end of the word *flu*. Point to each sound as you say it.

fl**u**

The letter o in the word *you* o is silent. Do you hear the "oo" at the end of the word *you*?

yo**u**

CULTIVATING READING AND PHONICS SKILLS 1ST GRADE – 3RD GRADE

3-D Flash Cards: **Long Vowel Sounds: Vowels on the End of Words and Syllables**
Student colors each letter with a **blue marker**.

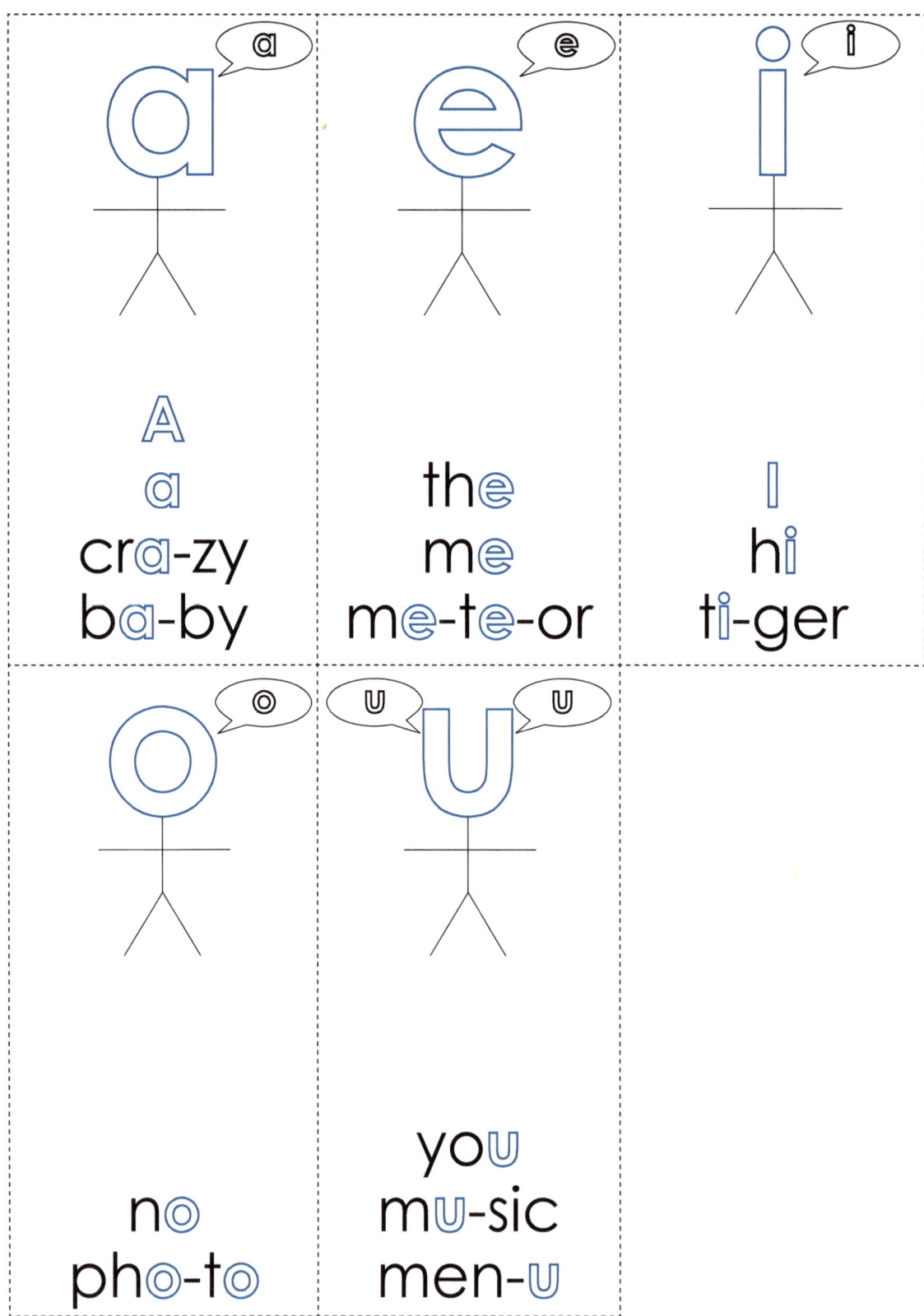

SPELL WORDS (10 TO 30 MINUTES)

MATERIALS – Yellow marker and **blue** pen

INSTRUCTOR SAYS – Use the blue pen to circle the vowels (a e i o u) in the alphabet on the following page.

For this activity, you will spell important words that end with long vowel sounds. **The purpose of this exercise is for you to say each word you spell so slowly that you can hear each sound as you write each letter.**

Spelling Words Long Vowel Sounds Vowels on the End of Words and Syllables
Long vowels say their names "a" "e" "i" "o" "u"
a he she me we the hi I no go so you (the o is silent)

DURING THIS ACTIVITY – Cover the spelling words, so your student can't see them. Provide immediate feedback for correct responses with stars or happy faces. More importantly, provide immediate feedback for all errors by writing the correct word with a yellow marker and **ask the student to trace over each letter while saying its corresponding sound.**

CULTIVATING READING AND PHONICS SKILLS 1ST GRADE – 3RD GRADE

 **EXPLAIN** – Look back over the words you spelled and draw stick figures under the letters that make the *long vowel* sounds with a *blue* pen.

Notice how each word follows the same pattern. The *long vowels are on the ends of each word*, and they all *say their names*.

 **NOTE for English language learners** – English language learners should sketch a drawing next to each word they spell, unless it is a word they already know. Talk about the meaning of each word. Afterwards, ask the student to create one sentence using two of the words. Model writing the sentence for the student with your yellow marker. Then ask the student to trace the yellow words.

Spell Long Vowel Sounds on the Ends of Words

abcdefghijklm
nopqrstuvwxyz

CULTIVATING READING AND PHONICS SKILLS 1ST GRADE – 3RD GRADE

MAKE 3-D FLASH CARDS FOR VOWEL TEAMS THAT HOLD HANDS (15 MINUTES)

MATERIALS – Visuals for the keywords; 3-D Flash Cards for **Long Vowel Sounds: Vowel Teams: ea ee ey ai ay oa ie ui ue** (See Appendix B); colored markers that include a **blue marker**

Vowel Teams That Hold Hands	Visual and Keyword
ai	rain
ay	spray
ea	beads
ee	tree
ey	key
ie	pie
oa	boat
ui	fruit juice
ue	blue glue

INSTRUCTOR SAYS – Let's review. What are the vowels? (**a**, **e**, **i**, **o**, **u**, and sometimes **y**). The letter **y** is a consonant when it makes the **yoyo** sound. If the letter **y** is not making the **yoyo** sound, then it is a vowel.

EXPLAIN – Remember every word must have a vowel. Also, there must be a vowel in every syllable.

Vowels can make different sounds. Short vowels make the **a**pple, **e**lephant, **i**gloo, **o**ctopus, and **u**mbrella sounds. What are the long vowel sounds? To hear the sounds that long vowels make, just say the names of each of these vowels.

a   e   i   o   u

A long vowel sound is the name of a vowel.

There are different ways we can spell **long a, e, i, o,** and **u** sounds in the English language.

We learned that one way to make long vowel sounds is when two vowels hold hands in a word. The vowels are *a*, *e*, *i*, *o*, *u*, and sometimes *y*. What are the names of the two vowels in the word **team**?

If I draw bodies on the vowels *e* and the *a*, you can see how they are next to each other and holding hands in the word **team**.

te**a**m

A vowel team is when two vowels team up in a word to make a long vowel sound. **In vowel teams, the long vowel sound is the name of the first vowel.**

Draw bodies on the vowels in the word **boat** below. The vowel team *oa* says, "*o*." Isn't *o* the name of a vowel?

The word **boat** is made up of three sounds. Point to each sound as you say it.

b   **oa**   t

Did you hear the **long o** sound? (If not, have the student try again.)

What are the long vowel sounds? (*a*, *e*, *i*, *o*, and *u*)
Each long vowel sound is the name of a vowel.

Now say the word **beads**. What long vowel sound do you hear in the word **beads**?

Draw bodies on the vowels.
Point to each sound as you say it.
Isn't *e* the name of a vowel?

b   **ea**   d   s

Draw bodies on the vowels in the words *fruit* and *juice* below.

Long a, e, i, and o have only one sound, but long u has two sounds. What long vowel sound do you hear in the word *juice*? Point to each sound as you say it.

j   **ui**   ce

What long vowel sound do you hear in the word *fruit*? Point to each sound as you say it.

fr   **ui**   t

CULTIVATING READING AND PHONICS SKILLS 1ST GRADE – 3RD GRADE

Remember, *long u* can make two sounds. It can say its name or say "oo" in words like *fruit* and *juice*. It can also say its name at the end of words like *menu.*

Remember to link the letter group you're learning to its keyword and visual. Why?

Anchoring spelling patterns to keywords and visuals can also help us distinguish the same sound when it is spelled differently. For example, the *long e* sound in the word *tree* is spelled differently from the *long e* sound in the word *beads*. Some words like *tree* use *ee* to spell the *long e* sound, other words like *beads*, use *ea* to spell the same sound.

Another reason to link the letter group to its keyword and visual is because later we will learn that some of the letter groups can make multiple sounds. For example, *ea* can make different sounds like *beads, steak*, and *feather.*

3-D Flash Cards: **Long Vowel Sounds: Vowel Teams: ea ee ey ai ay oa ie ui ue**
Student colors letter groups with a **blue marker** then draws the keyword for each card.

CULTIVATING READING AND PHONICS SKILLS 1ST GRADE – 3RD GRADE

3-D Flash Cards: **Long Vowel Sounds: Vowel Teams: ea ee ey ai ay oa ie ui ue**
Student colors letter groups with a **blue marker** then draws the keyword for each card.

IDENTIFY AND HIGHLIGHT VOWEL TEAMS (10 MINUTES)

MATERIALS – "The Beast" passage below; the student's 3-D Flash Cards; yellow marker

INSTRUCTOR SAYS – Look at the passage below. Look at each word and highlight with a yellow marker the **long e** vowel teams holding hands (**ee** and **ea**).

The Beast

I dream of a beast.
I dream of a beast in the sea.

I scream!
I scream, and it leaps!
"EEEEK!"

It leaps and weeps.
I feel sad for the beast.

I speak to him in the dream.
He tells me his name is Steve.
He is sweet.

I was a creep.
I was a creep to scream.

He is not a beast.
Who is the beast? Me.

 **EXPLAIN** – Point to the word **Beast** in the title of the story.

What does **ea** sound like in the word **Beast**? The vowels **e** and **a** are side by side, and they are holding hands, aren't they? Find your 3-D Flash Card for **ea** with the keyword **beads**.

What about the words **me** and **the** (POINT TO)? In both these words, remember when the vowel is on the end of a word or syllable, it can also make a long vowel sound. Find your 3-D Flash Card for **e** with the keyword **the**, **me**, and **me-te-or**.

Look at the word **Steve**. It has two **e**'s. The first one says the long e sound, but the second **e** in **Steve** is silent. We'll learn more about **silent e** next.

And what about the word **tell** (POINT TO)? The **e** is not holding hands with another vowel, is it? So, the **e** in this word makes the same short e sound that's in **elephant**. Find the short e flash card.

CULTIVATING READING AND PHONICS SKILLS 1ST GRADE – 3RD GRADE

INSTRUCTOR SAYS – Next, we will read this story in the book. As you read the story, you can refer back to these highlighted words. We can use Dot Time or your flash cards to figure out some of the words. We'll also write down words, on your Round Up paper, that don't follow patterns you've learned.

READ AND SPELL WORDS FROM THE STORY (10 TO 30 MINUTES)

MATERIALS – "The Beast" in the book, *Phonics Stories: Long Vowels,* by Laurie Hunter; the student's 3-D Flash Cards; Dot Time stickers; Spotlighting penlight; yellow marker; **blue** and **pink** pens

AT THE BEGINNING OF EVERY SESSION – Review the student's 3-D Flash Cards.

WHILE READING EACH STORY – Allow the student to practice blending difficult words using the 3-D Flash Cards, Dot Time, and/or Spotlighting.

NOTE – If the student made three or more errors while reading the story, then have the student reread the story again to build word recognition and fluency. The student should reread and master each story before progressing to the next one.

INSTRUCTOR SAYS – For this activity, I will select seven **long e** words and one **short e** word (**tell**) for you to spell. **The purpose of this exercise is for you to say each word you spell so slowly that you can hear each sound as you write each letter.**

Spell Long e and Short e Words from "The Beast"				
the	beast	weep	Steve	tell
he	dream	feel		
me	sea	sweet		
	scream	creep		
	leaps			
	speak			

DURING THIS ACTIVITY – Cover the spelling words, so your student can't see them. Provide immediate feedback for correct responses with stars or happy faces. More importantly, provide immediate feedback for all errors by writing the correct word with a yellow marker and **ask the student to trace over each letter while saying its corresponding sound.**

EXPLAIN – Look over all the words you spelled. Draw stick figures under the letters that make the *long e* sound with *blue* pen. Then draw a stick figure under the **e** in the word **tell** with a *pink* pen. It makes the *short e* sound. The **e**'s in **me** and **the** are long.

NOTE for English language learners – English language learners should sketch a drawing next to each word they spell, unless it is a word they already know. Talk about the meaning of each word. Afterwards, ask the student to create one sentence using two of the words. Model writing the sentence for the student with your yellow marker. Then ask the student to trace the yellow words.

CULTIVATING READING AND PHONICS SKILLS 1ST GRADE – 3RD GRADE

Spell Long e and Short e Words

headline
armline
footline

a b c d e f g h i j k l m

n o p q r s t u v w x y z

LAURIE HUNTER

INTRODUCE VOWEL TEAMS THAT JUMP ROPE (15 MINUTES)

MATERIALS – There are no visuals; 3-D Flash Cards for the Long Vowel Sounds: Vowel Teams: vowel-consonant-*silent e* (See Appendix B); a blue marker

Vowel Teams That Jump Rope (V-C-silent e)	Keywords
a_e	cake
e_e	gene
i_e	bike
o_e	hole
u_e	mule

INSTRUCTOR SAYS – Look at your *silent e* flash card. Notice how the vowels *a e i o* and *u* can team up with *silent e*. The first vowel says its name and the *e* is silent. Trace inside the *e* with the blue marker.

EXPLAIN – Let's make vowels stand out by drawing vowels with stick figure bodies. When we do this, we can bring vowels to life and see more clearly what is going on inside each word. Vowel teams can jump rope to make long vowel sounds.

Remember in the word **pie**, the *i* and the *e* are Vowel Teams Holding Hands.

In the word **pike**, the *i* and the *silent e* are Vowel Teams that Jump Rope. There is only 1 consonant between the vowels.

In the word **pickle**, there is more than 1 consonant between the *i* and the *silent e*, so the *i* and the *e* can't hold hands, nor can they jump rope. So, the *i* makes the *igloo* sound, the first sound we learned for *i*.

CULTIVATING READING AND PHONICS SKILLS 1ST GRADE – 3RD GRADE

In the word **pick**, the *i* is not teaming up with another vowel either, so the *i* makes the *igloo* sound.

3-D Flash Cards: **Long Vowel Sounds: Vowel Teams: vowel-consonant-*silent e***
The student traces inside each outlined letter with a **blue marker** while saying each long vowel sounds.

IDENTIFY AND HIGHLIGHT VOWEL TEAMS (10 MINUTES)

MATERIALS – "I Can Ride Nine Bikes at One Time" passage below; student's 3-D Flash Cards, yellow marker

INSTRUCTOR SAYS – Look at the passage below. Look at each word and highlight with a yellow marker the **long i** vowel teams that are holding hands (**ie**), jumping rope (**i_e**) and **long i** on the end of words.

I Can Ride Nine Bikes at One Time

I can ride.
I can ride nine bikes.
I can ride nine bikes at one time!

I lied.
I tried to ride nine bikes at one time.
I died!
Yikes!

I lied.
I did not die.
I tried to ride nine bikes at one time and I *almost* died.

So I ride five bikes at one time, and I am fine!

EXPLAIN – Point to the word **ride** in the story.

Let's make the word **ride** with your 3-D Flash Cards. Use the **long i** and the **silent e** flash cards.
What is the **i** going to sound like in the word **ride**? (the **long i** sound, the **i** says its name)
And what sound does the **e** make? (It is silent, it doesn't say anything)
The **i** and the **e** are two vowels that are jumping rope, aren't they?

And what about the word **lied** (POINT TO)? What sound does the letter group **i** make in this word? (The **long i** sound, the **i** says its name and the **e** doesn't say anything.)
Let's make the word **lied** with your 3-D Flash Cards.

CULTIVATING READING AND PHONICS SKILLS 1ST GRADE – 3RD GRADE

And what about the word **did** (POINT TO)? The **i** is not holding hands with another vowel, is it? So, the *i* in this word makes the same short i sound that's in **igloo**. Find the short i flash card.

INSTRUCTOR SAYS – Next, we will read this story in the book. As you read the story, you can refer back to these highlighted words. We can also use Dot Time or your flash cards to figure out some of the words. We'll also write down words, on your Round Up paper, that don't follow patterns we've learned.

READ AND SPELL WORDS FROM THE STORY (10 TO 30 MINUTES)

MATERIALS – "I Can Ride Nine Bikes at One Time" in the book, *Phonics Stories: Long Vowels*, by Laurie Hunter; the student's 3-D Flash Cards; Spotlighting penlight; yellow marker; blue and pink pens.

AT THE BEGINNING OF EVERY SESSION – Review the student's 3-D Flash Cards.

WHILE READING EACH STORY – Allow the student to practice blending difficult words using the 3-D Flash Cards and Spotlighting.

NOTE – If the student made three or more errors while reading the story, then have the student read the story once again to build word recognition and fluency. The student should reread and master each story before progressing to the next one.

INSTRUCTOR SAYS – For this activity, I will select seven **long i** words and one **short i** word (**did**) from the story for you to spell. **The purpose of this exercise is for you to say each word you spell so slowly that you can hear each sound as you write each letter.**

Spell Long i and Short i Words from "I Can Ride Nine Bikes at One Time"			
I	lied tried died die	ride nine bikes time yikes! five fine	did

DURING THIS ACTIVITY – Cover the spelling words, so your student can't see them. Provide immediate feedback for correct responses with stars or happy faces. More importantly, provide immediate feedback for all errors by writing the correct word with a yellow marker and **ask the student to trace over each letter while saying its corresponding sound**.

EXPLAIN – Look over all the words you spelled. Draw stick figures under the letters that make the *long i* sound with *blue* pen. Then draw a stick figure under the *i* in the word *did* with a *pink* pen. It makes the *short i* sound. The *i* in the word *I* is *long*.

NOTE for English language learners – English language learners should sketch a drawing next to each word they spell, unless it is a word they already know. Talk about the meaning of each word. Afterwards, ask the student to create one sentence using two of the words. Model writing the sentence for the student with your yellow marker. Then ask the student to trace the yellow words.

CULTIVATING READING AND PHONICS SKILLS 1ST GRADE – 3RD GRADE

Spell Long i and Short i Words

abcdefghijklm
nopqrstuvwxyz

IDENTIFY AND HIGHLIGHT VOWEL TEAMS (10 MINUTES)

 **MATERIALS** – "Spain" passage below; the student's 3-D Flash Cards; yellow marker

 **INSTRUCTOR SAYS** – Look at the passage below. Look at each word and highlight with a yellow marker the **long a** vowel teams (**ai** and **ay**), the **long a** vowel team jumping rope (**a_e**), and **long a** on the end of words or syllables.

Spain

One day, Steve set sail.
One day, Steve set sail to Spain.
In Spain, he takes a train to a trail.

He takes the trail to a cave.
In the cave, he is lost
Steve gets his map.

With the map, he makes his way.
He makes his way in the cave.

In the cave, he sees shapes (formations):
a brain, tail, snake, and snail!

Rain water made its way to the cave and made the shapes.
The rain water made the brain, tail, snake, and snail.
It was amazing!

 **EXPLAIN** – Point to the word **Spain** in the title of the story.

What is the **ai** going to sound like in this word? (the **long a** sound, the *a* says its name)

The *a* and the *i* are two vowels that are side by side in the word. They are holding hands, aren't they? The two vowels are teaming up to make the *a* say, "*a*."

And what about this word **takes**? The *a* and the **silent e** are two vowels that are jumping rope with the consonant **k**, aren't they? The **silent e** makes the *a* say, "*a*."

CULTIVATING READING AND PHONICS SKILLS 1ST GRADE – 3RD GRADE

INSTRUCTOR SAYS – Next, we will read this story in the book. As you read the story, you can refer back to these highlighted words. We can use Dot Time or your flash cards to figure out some of the words. We'll also write down words, on your Round Up paper, that don't follow patterns you've learned.

READ AND SPELL WORDS FROM THE STORY (10 TO 20 MINUTES)

MATERIALS – "Spain" in the book, *Phonics Stories: Long Vowels,* by Laurie Hunter; the student's 3-D Flash Cards; Dot Time stickers; Spotlighting penlight; yellow marker; **blue** and **pink** pens

AT THE BEGINNING OF EVERY SESSION – Review the student's 3-D Flash Cards.

WHILE READING EACH STORY – Allow the student to practice blending difficult words using the 3-D Flash Cards, Dot Time, and/or Spotlighting.

NOTE – If the student made three or more errors while reading the story, then have the student read the story once again to build word recognition and fluency. The student should reread and master each story before progressing to the next one.

INSTRUCTOR SAYS – For this activity, I will select seven **long a** words and one **short a** word (**and, had, or back**) from the story for you to spell. **The purpose of this exercise is for you to say each word you spell so slowly that you can hear each sound as you write each letter**.

Spell Long a and Short a Words from "Spain"				
a for-ma-tions a-ma-zing	day way	Spain sail train trail brain tail snail rain	takes cave makes shapes snake made	map and

DURING THIS ACTIVITY – Cover the spelling words, so your student can't see them. Provide immediate feedback for correct responses with stars or happy faces. More importantly, provide immediate feedback for all errors by writing the correct word with a yellow marker and **ask the student to trace over each letter while saying its corresponding sound**.

EXPLAIN – Look over all the words you spelled. Draw stick figures under the letters that make the *long a* sound with *blue* pen. Then draw a stick figure under the **a** in the word **and, had**, or **back** with a *pink* pen. It makes the *short a* sound. The **a**'s in **a**, **for-ma-tions**, and **a-ma-zing** are *long*.

NOTE for English language learners – English language learners should sketch a drawing next to each word they spell, unless it is a word they already know. Talk about the meaning of each word. Afterwards, ask the student to create one sentence using two of the words. Model writing the sentence for the student with your yellow marker. Then ask the student to trace the yellow words.

CULTIVATING READING AND PHONICS SKILLS 1ST GRADE – 3RD GRADE

Spell Long a and Short a Words

headline
armline
footline

a b c d e f g h i j k l m

n o p q r s t u v w x y z

IDENTIFY AND HIGHLIGHT VOWEL TEAMS (10 MINUTES)

MATERIALS – "Home" passage below; student's 3-D Flash Cards; yellow marker

INSTRUCTOR SAYS – Look at the passage below. Look at each word and highlight with a yellow marker the **long o** vowel team (**oa**), the **long o** vowel team jumping rope (**o_e**), and **long o** on the end of words.

Home

Steve likes to roam.
Steve roams the globe.
He drove a boat.
He drove a boat to the coast of Mexico.

On the coast of Mexico, he saw beautiful beaches.
On the coast, he saw homes of Mayans that lived long ago.

He swam with beautiful fish and saw their homes of coral.

He saw beautiful mangrove trees.
Mangrove trees are home to so many animals and fish.
The mangrove trees clean the water and air.

Steve had fun, but he hopes to go back to his home!

EXPLAIN – Point to the word **roam** in the story.

What is the **oa** going to sound like in this word? (the **long o** sound, the **o** says its name)

The **o** and **a** are two vowels that are side by side in the word. They are holding hands, aren't they?

And what about this word **home**? The **o** and the **silent e** are jumping rope with the consonant **m**, aren't they?

And what about this word **so**? The **o** is at the end of the word, isn't it? Yes, the **o** in this word will also say its name.

CULTIVATING READING AND PHONICS SKILLS 1ST GRADE – 3RD GRADE

And what about the word **on** (POINT TO)? The **o** is not holding hands with another vowel, is it? So, the **o** in this word makes the same short o sound that's in **o**ctopus. Find the short o flash card.

INSTRUCTOR SAYS – Next, we will read this story in the book. As you read the story, you can refer back to these highlighted words. We can use Spotlighting or your flash cards to figure out some of the words. We'll also write down words, on your Round Up paper, that don't follow patterns you've learned.

READ AND SPELL WORDS FROM THE STORY (10 TO 30 MINUTES)

MATERIALS – "Home" in the book, *Phonics Stories: Long Vowels*, by Laurie Hunter; the student's 3-D Flash Cards; Spotlighting penlight; yellow marker; blue and pink pens

AT THE BEGINNING OF EVERY SESSION – Review the student's 3-D Flash Cards.

WHILE READING EACH STORY – Allow the student to practice blending difficult words using the 3-D Flash Cards or Spotlighting.

NOTE – If the student made three or more errors while reading the story, then have the student read the story once again to build word recognition and fluency. The student should reread and master each story before progressing to the next one.

INSTRUCTOR SAYS – For this activity, I will select seven **long o** words and one **short o** word (**on**) for you to spell. **The purpose of this exercise is for you to say each word you spell so slowly that you can hear each sound as you write each letter.**

Spell Long o and Short o Words from "Home"			
Mex-i-co	roam	home	on
a-go	roams	homes	long
so	boat	globe	
go	coast	drove	
		man-grove	
		hopes	

DURING THIS ACTIVITY – Cover the spelling words, so student can't see them. Provide immediate feedback for correct responses with stars or happy faces. More importantly, provide immediate feedback for all errors by writing the correct word with a yellow marker and **ask student to trace over each letter while saying its corresponding sound**.

EXPLAIN – Look over all the words you spelled. Draw stick figures under the letters that make the *long o* sound with a *blue* pen. Then draw a stick figure under the **o** in the word **on** with a *pink* pen. It makes the *short o* sound. The **o**'s in **Mexico**, **ago**, **so**, and **go** are *long*.

NOTE for English language learners – English language learners should sketch a drawing next to each word they spell, unless it is a word they already know. Talk about the meaning of each word. Afterwards, ask the student to create one sentence using two of the words. Model writing the sentence for the student with your yellow marker. Then ask the student to trace the yellow words.

CULTIVATING READING AND PHONICS SKILLS 1ST GRADE – 3RD GRADE

Spell Long o and Short o Sounds

headline
armline
footline

a b c d e f g h i j k l m

n o p q r s t u v w x y z

IDENTIFY AND HIGHLIGHT VOWEL TEAMS (10 MINUTES)

MATERIALS – "The Flu" passage below; *the student*'s 3-D Flash Cards; yellow marker

INSTRUCTOR SAYS – Look at the passage below. Look inside each word and highlight with a yellow marker the **long u** vowel teams (**ue** and **ui**), the **long u** vowel team jumping rope (**u_e**), and **long u** on the end of words.

The Flu

Steve was sick.
Steve was sick with the flu.
"Achoo!"

His doctor was Dr. Sue.
Dr. Sue took care of Steve.

Steve had to be in a cube.
He had to be in a cube, so others did not get his flu.

Steve had a cute blue mask.
Dr. Sue gave him fruit juice.
The fruit juice was blue too.

Soon, Steve felt better.
No more flu!
No more cube!

Steve gave Dr. Sue a huge "Thank You!"
He still uses cute blue masks and washes his hands often.
How about you?

EXPLAIN – Point to the word **Sue** in the story.

What is the **ue** going to sound like in this word? Remember the **long u** has two sounds.

Long a, e, i, and o have only one sound, but *long u* has two sounds. It can say its name **u** or it can say /oo/ like you hear in the word **Sue**. Point to each sound as you say it.

CULTIVATING READING AND PHONICS SKILLS 1ST GRADE – 3RD GRADE

S **ue**

And what about this word **cube**? The **u** and the **e** are jumping rope with the consonant **b**, aren't they?

What long vowel sound do you hear in the word **cube**? Point to each sound as you say it.

c **u** b **e**

Long u can sound like "oo" in **Sue** and like "u" in **cube**.

Remember also that **a vowel at the end of a word or syllable is another way to make a vowel say its name**. Do you hear the **u** say, "oo" in this word? Point to each sound as you say it. Remember **long u** has two, sounds "u" and "oo."

f l **u**

READ AND SPELL WORDS FROM THE STORY (10 TO 30 MINUTES)

MATERIALS – "The Flu" in the book, *Phonics Stories: Long Vowels*, by Laurie Hunter; *the* student's 3-D Flash Cards; Spotlighting penlight; yellow marker; **blue** and **pink** pens.

AT THE BEGINNING OF EVERY SESSION – Review the student's 3-D Flash Cards.

WHILE READING EACH STORY – Allow the student to practice blending difficult words using the 3-D Flash Cards and Spotlighting.

NOTE – If the student made three or more errors while reading the story, then have the student read the story once again to build word recognition and fluency. The student should reread and master each story before progressing to the next one.

INSTRUCTOR SAYS – For this activity, I will select eight **long u** words from the story for you to spell. **The purpose of this exercise is for you to say each word you spell so slowly that you can hear each sound as you write each letter.**

Spell Long u Words from "The Flu"			
flu	Sue	cube	achoo!
you (o is silent)	blue	cute	too
	fruit	huge	soon
	juice	uses	

DURING THIS ACTIVITY – Cover the spelling words, so your student can't see them. Provide immediate feedback for correct responses with stars or happy faces. More importantly, provide immediate feedback for all errors by writing the correct word with a yellow marker and **ask the student to trace over each letter while saying its corresponding sound**.

EXPLAIN – Look over all the words you spelled. Draw stick figures under the letters that make the *long u* sound with a *blue* pen.

NOTE for English language learners – English language learners should sketch a drawing next to each word they spell, unless it is a word they already know. Talk about the meaning of each word. Afterwards, ask the student to create one sentence using two of the words. Model writing the sentence for the student with your yellow marker. Then ask the student to trace the yellow words.

CULTIVATING READING AND PHONICS SKILLS 1ST GRADE – 3RD GRADE

Spell Long u Words

headline
armline
footline

a b c d e f g h i j k l m
n o p q r s t u v w x y z

STEP 5 | EXPLAIN SOFT C AND G

> *I find that the great thing in this world is not so much where we stand, as in what direction we are moving.*
>
> Oliver Wendell Holmes

MAKE 3-D FLASH CARDS FOR THE OTHER CONSONANT SOUNDS FOR C AND G (10 MINUTES)

MATERIALS – Visuals for the keywords; 3-D Flash Cards for the **Consonant Sounds: Soft c and g** (See Appendix B); and a **green marker**

Hard & Soft c and g	Visual and Keyword
hard c	cat
soft c	cereal
hard g	gum
soft g	giraffe

INSTRUCTOR SAYS – You've probably noticed by now that the letters **c** and **g** have two sounds. Take a look at the Flash Cards for **c** and **g**. Trace inside the **c** and **g** with the green marker.

EXPLAIN – The letter **c** will **always** make /s/ in **cereal** when **c** is followed by **e, i,** or **y**. When **c** is followed by any other letter it always makes the /k/ sound in **cat**. Take a look at these words and listen for the /s/ sound.

ce	ci	cy
cent	citrus	juicy
face	city	icy
rice	circus	bicycle

CULTIVATING READING AND PHONICS SKILLS 1ˢᵀ GRADE – 3ᴿᴰ GRADE

The letter **g** sometimes, *not always*, sounds like /j/ in **jam** and **jelly** when **g** is followed by **e, i**, or **y**.

ge	gi	gy
gem	giant	gym
gel	rigid	edgy
change	gigantic	Egypt

3-D Flash Cards: **Consonant Sounds: Soft c and g**
The student colors the outlined letters with a **green marker**. Student does not need to draw the keyword for each letter.

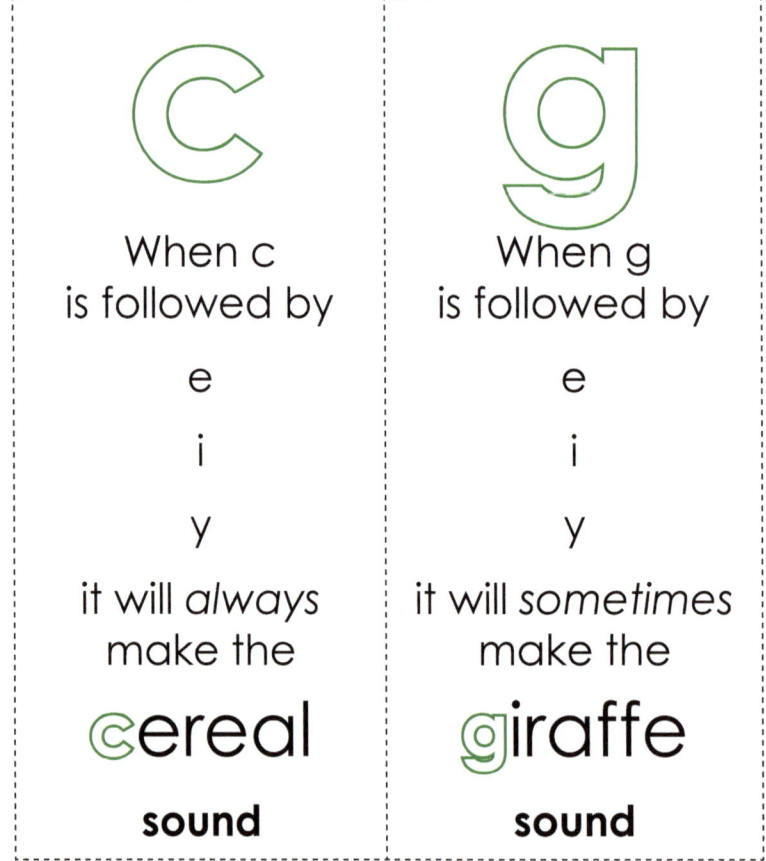

IDENTIFY AND HIGHLIGHT SOFT C (10 MINUTES)

 **MATERIALS** – "Mice in the City" passage below; the student's 3-D Flash Cards; yellow marker

 **INSTRUCTOR SAYS** – Look at the passage below. Look at each word and highlight with a yellow marker the **c**'s that make the **cereal** sound (**ce ci cy**). Next, find the word **gym** and highlight with a yellow marker the **g**'s.

Mice in the City

Steve misses his friends.
His friends are mice.
The mice live in the city.

Steve rides his bike to see the mice.
The mice ride on his bicycle.
They ride his bicycle in the big city.

They ride his bike to the gym.
Steve and the mice dance in gym class.
They dance and prance.

Ater gym class, they like to eat.
The mice eat rice and ice cream.
Yum!

After eating rice and ice cream, they dance again.
It puts a smile on their face.
It is nice to dance and eat ice cream with friends!

 **EXPLAIN** – The letter **c** will always make the **cereal** sound when **c** is followed by an **e**, **i**, or **y**. If **c** is followed by any other letter it will make the **cat** sound.

What sound does the **c** make in the word **raced**? The **c** is followed by an **e**, so it will make the **cereal** sound, right?

When there is an **e** after the **c**, it will make the /s/ sound like it does in the word **cereal**.

CULTIVATING READING AND PHONICS SKILLS 1ST GRADE – 3RD GRADE

Point to the word **city** in the title of the story. The **c** is followed by an **i**, so that's why the **c** in **city** makes the /s/ sound. Point to each sound as you say it.

c i

  ci t

    cit y

      city

The **c** will make the /s/ sound in the word below also. Point to each sound as you say it.

d a n

  dan **ce**

    dan**c**e

In the word **class**, the **c** is not followed by an **e**, **i**, or **y**, so it will make the **cat** sound. Point to each sound as you say it.

c l

  cl a

    cla ss

So tell me again, why does this **c** in **class** make the **cat** sound and not the **cereal** sound? (Because there is not an **e**, **i**, or **y** after the **c**, so it will make the **cat** sound.)

INSTRUCTOR SAYS – Next, we will read this story in the book. As you read the story, you can refer back to these highlighted words. We can also use Dot Time or your flash cards to figure out some of the words. We'll also write down words, on your Round Up paper, that don't follow patterns we've learned.

READ AND SPELL WORDS FROM THE STORY (10 TO 20 MINUTES)

MATERIALS – "Mice in the City" in the book *Phonics Stories: Long Vowels*; the student's 3-D Flash Cards, Dot Time stickers, Spotlighting penlight, yellow marker, and **green** pen

LAURIE HUNTER

AT THE BEGINNING OF EVERY SESSION – Review the student's 3-D Flash Cards.

WHILE READING EACH STORY – Allow the student to practice blending difficult words using the 3-D Flash Cards, Dot Time, and/or Spotlighting.

NOTE – If the student made three or more errors while reading the story, then have the student read the story once again to build word recognition and fluency. The student should reread and master each story before progressing to the next one.

INSTRUCTOR SAYS – For this activity, I will select seven soft *c* and *g* words for you to spell. **The purpose of this exercise is for you to say each word you spell so slowly that you can hear each sound as you write each letter.**

Spell soft c and g Words from "Mice in the City"				
c	ce	ci	cy	gy
class cream	mice dance prance rice ice face nice	city	bicycle	gym

EXPLAIN – Now look over all the words you spelled and trace over the *c*'s followed by *e*, *i*, or *y* with a green marker. Now look over all the words you spelled and trace over the *g*'s followed by *y* with a green marker. Notice how each word follows a pattern.

NOTE for English language learners – English language learners should sketch a drawing next to each word they spell, unless it is a word they already know. Talk about the meaning of each word. Afterwards, ask the student to create one sentence using two of the words. Model writing the sentence for the student with your yellow marker. Then ask the student to trace the yellow words.

CULTIVATING READING AND PHONICS SKILLS 1ST GRADE – 3RD GRADE

Spell Soft c and g Words

a b c d e f g h i j k l m
n o p q r s t u v w x y z

STEP 6 | **TEACH *THE OTHER* VOWEL SOUNDS**

> *"Challenges are what make life interesting; overcoming them is what makes life meaningful."*
>
> Joshua L. Marine

MAKE 3-D FLASH CARDS FOR *THE OTHER* VOWEL SOUNDS (10 MINUTES)

 **MATERIALS** – Visuals for the keywords; 3-D Flash Cards for *The Other* Vowel Sounds (See Appendix B); colored markers that include an orange marker

 **INSTRUCTOR SAYS** – First, we studied short vowel sounds, then we studied long vowel sounds.

What are the short vowel sounds?

/a/ as in **a**pple

/e/ **e**lephant

/i/ **i**gloo

/o/ **o**ctopus

/u/ **u**mbrella

What are the long vowel sounds?

a, *e*, *i*, *o*, *u*. The long vowel sounds are the names of the vowels.

Now, we're going to study *The Other* Vowel Sounds. We'll call them "*The Other* Vowel Sounds" because they do not make long or short vowel sounds.

CULTIVATING READING AND PHONICS SKILLS 1ST GRADE – 3RD GRADE

The Other Vowel Sounds	Visual and Keyword
ow	cow
ou	mouse
oi	coin
oy	boy
oo	book
ar	star
or	fork
ur	purple
ir	shirt
er	certificate

EXPLAIN – What sound do the letters **ow** make in the word **cow**? Can you hear the **o** make the **octopus** sound? (no) Can you hear the **w** make the **watch** sound? No, they make the /ow!/ sound; **ow!** is short for **ouch!**

The **o** and **w** mix together to make a whole new sound, just like you can mix red and yellow paint to make another color, orange.

We can distinguish spelling differences in similar sounds such as **ow** and **ou**. For example, the /ow!/ sound in **flower**, the plant, is spelled like **cow**. The /ow!/ sound in **flour**, the kind I cook with, is spelled like **mouse**.

ou, **oi**, **oy**, and **oo** are not vowel teams. Why not? Because, the **o** in **mouse**, **coin**, **boy**, and **book** does not say its name.

Remember a vowel team is two vowels that team up in a word to make a long vowel sound. The only **long o** vowel team is **oa**, like in the keyword **boat**.

The Other Vowel Sounds are not long or short. They are letter groups that make other vowel sounds. We'll learn all the spelling patterns with each story we read.

3-D Flash Cards: **The Other** Vowel Sounds: **oi oy ow ou oo ar or ur ir er**
Student colors letter groups with an **orange marker** then draws the keywords.

CULTIVATING READING AND PHONICS SKILLS 1ST GRADE – 3RD GRADE

3-D Flash Cards: *The Other* Vowel Sounds: oi oy ow ou oo ar or ur ir er
Student colors letter groups with an orange marker then draws the keywords.

LAURIE HUNTER

IDENTIFY AND HIGHLIGHT *THE OTHER* VOWEL SOUNDS (10 MINUTES)

 **MATERIALS** – "The Brave Brown Cow" passage below; yellow marker

 **INSTRUCTOR SAYS** – Look at the passage below. Look inside each word and highlight with a yellow marker the **ou** and **ow**'s.

The Brave Cow And Mouse

One day a cow heard a loud shout.
The cow heard someone shout, "Help! I am drowning!"

The cow looked around.
She saw a brown mouse drowning in the town lake.

The cow bounced from the ground into the lake.
The brave cow swam to the mouse drowning in the lake.
The brown mouse got on the cow's back.

They got out of the lake and on to the ground.
The brown mouse found his mom in the crowd.
His mom thanked the brave cow.
"Thank you!"

The cow was so proud.
She had saved the mouse!

 **EXPLAIN** – The **ou** and **ow** make the /ow!/ sound. "**Ow!**" is the shortened form of the word "**Ouch!**" Highlight with yellow marker, all /ow!/ sounds (**ou** and **ow**) on the worksheet.

Point to the word **drowning** in the story.

What is the **ow** going to sound like in the word **drowning**?

Point to each sound as you say it.

CULTIVATING READING AND PHONICS SKILLS 1ST GRADE – 3RD GRADE

d r **ow**

    dr**ow** n

        dr**ow** ing

-ing on the end of words means that it is happening now.

Point to the word **bounced** in the story.

What is the **ou** going to sound like in the word **bounced**?

b **ou**

    b**ou** n

        b**ou**n **ce**

            b**ou**n**ce** d

-d on the end of this word means that it happened in the past.

Also, the letter **c** is followed by **silent e**. When **c** is followed by an **e**, **i**, or **y**, it makes the **cereal** /s/ sound. If **c** is followed by any other letter, it makes the **cat** sound.

There are two ways we spell the /ow!/ sound in English. Words like **dr*ow*ning**, **br*ow*n**, and **c*ow*** use **ow** and words like m**ou**se and b**ou**nced use **ou**.

READ AND SPELL WORDS FROM THE STORY (10 TO 20 MINUTES)

MATERIALS – "The Brave Brown Cow" story, in the book, *Phonics Stories: Long Vowels*, by Laurie Hunter; the student's 3-D Flash Cards; Dot stickers; Spotlighting penlight; yellow marker and **orange marker**

AT THE BEGINNING OF EVERY SESSION – Review the student's 3-D Flash Cards.

READ THE STORY – As the student reads the story, use the 3-D Flash Cards, Dot Time, or Spotlighting to help the student figure out difficult words.

NOTE – If the student made three or more errors while reading the story, then have the student read the story once again to build word recognition and fluency. The student should reread and master each story before progressing to the next one.

INSTRUCTOR SAYS – For this activity, you'll spell seven **ou and ow** words from the story. **The purpose of this exercise is for you to say each word you spell so slowly that you can hear each sound as you write each letter**.

Spell ow and ou Words from "The Brave Brown Cow"	
brown	loud
cow	shout
crowd	around
drown	mouse
drown-ing	bounce
town	bounce-d
	ground
	proud

DURING THIS ACTIVITY – Cover the spelling words, so your student can't see them. Provide immediate feedback for correct responses with stars or happy faces. More importantly, provide immediate feedback for all errors by writing the correct word with a yellow marker and **ask the student to trace over each letter while saying its corresponding sound**.

EXPLAIN – Look over all the words you spelled. Trace over the letters *ou* and *ow* with orange marker. The /ow!/ sound is spelled two different ways, but both spellings make the same sound.

NOTE for English language learners – English language learners should sketch a drawing next to each word they spell, unless it is a word they already know. Talk about the meaning of each word. Afterwards, ask the student to create one sentence using two of the words. Model writing the sentence for the student with your yellow marker. Then ask the student to trace the yellow words.

CULTIVATING READING AND PHONICS SKILLS 1ST GRADE – 3RD GRADE

Spell *The Other* Vowel Sounds from "The Brave Cow and Mouse"

headline
armline
footline

a b c d e f g h i j k l m

n o p q r s t u v w x y z

IDENTIFY AND HIGHLIGHT *THE OTHER* VOWEL SOUNDS (10 MINUTES)

MATERIALS – "Little Hoof" passage below; yellow marker

INSTRUCTOR SAYS – Look at the passage below. Look inside each word and highlight with a yellow marker the **oo**'s.

Little Hoof

There once was a little pony.
The little pony had a red cape and hood.
No, her name was not Little Red Riding Hood.
Her name was Little Hoof.

Little Hoof took a walk in the woods.
She took a walk in the woods to her grandmother's house.
Little Hoof cooked lunch for her grandmother.
After she cooked lunch, she read her grandmother a book.

Her grandmother thanked Little Hoof.
She thanked her for cooking lunch and reading a book.

EXPLAIN – Point to the word **hoof** in the title.

What is the **oo** going to sound like in the word **hoof**?

Point to each sound as you say it.

h oo f

h oo d

w oo d

CULTIVATING READING AND PHONICS SKILLS 1ST GRADE – 3RD GRADE

READ AND SPELL WORDS FROM THE STORY (10 TO 20 MINUTES)

MATERIALS – "Little Hoof" in the book, *Phonics Stories: Long Vowels*, by Laurie Hunter; *the* student's 3-D Flash Cards; Dot stickers; Spotlighting penlight; orange marker

AT THE BEGINNING OF EVERY SESSION – Review the student's 3-D Flash Cards.

READ THE STORY – As the student reads the story, use the 3-D Flash Cards, Dot Time, or Spotlighting to help the student figure out difficult words.

NOTE – If the student made three or more errors while reading the story, then have the student read the story once again to build word recognition and fluency. The student should reread and master each story before progressing to the next one.

INSTRUCTOR SAYS – For this activity, I will select eight **oo** words from the story. **The purpose of this exercise is for you to say each word you spell so slowly that you can hear each sound as you write each letter.**

Spell oo Words from "Little Hoof"
hoof
hood
wood
woods
cook
cook-ed
cook-ing
book

DURING THIS ACTIVITY – Cover the spelling words, so your student can't see them. Provide immediate feedback for correct responses with stars or happy faces. More importantly, provide immediate feedback for all errors by writing the correct word with a yellow marker and **ask the student to trace over each letter while saying its corresponding sound.**

EXPLAIN – Look over all the words you spelled. Trace over the letters **oo** that make the /oo/ sound in **book** with orange marker. You may already know that the letters **oo** make another sound you hear in the word **moon**, but we will talk about that and make the Flash Card for **moon** later.

144

 **NOTE for English language learners** – English language learners should sketch a drawing next to each word they spell, unless it is a word they already know. Talk about the meaning of each word. Afterwards, ask the student to create one sentence using two of the words. Model writing the sentence for the student with your yellow marker. Then ask the student to trace the yellow words.

CULTIVATING READING AND PHONICS SKILLS 1ST GRADE – 3RD GRADE

Spell *The Other* Vowel Sounds from "Little Hoof"

headline
armline
footline

abcdefghijklm

nopqrstuvwxyz

LAURIE HUNTER

IDENTIFY AND HIGHLIGHT *THE OTHER* VOWEL SOUNDS (10 MINUTES)

 **MATERIALS** – "Bart from Mars" passage below; yellow marker

 **INSTRUCTOR SAYS** – Look at the passage below. Look inside each word and highlight with a yellow marker the **ar**.

Bart from Mars

Bart is on Mars.
Bart is on Mars, but he dreams of going to Earth.

Bart dreams of going to a park.
He dreams of driving a car and seeing sharks.

But he cannot go to Earth and drive a car
or go to a park
or see sharks
because he is far away on the planet Mars.
He wished upon a star.

Bart is smart.
After his wish, he learned how to make a car on Mars.
And he made a park on Mars!

But, there are no sharks on Mars.
So, he made art and put sharks in his art.
And he still dreams of going to Earth!

 **EXPLAIN** – Point to the word **Bart** in the title of the story.

Bart is the name of a character in the story. What sound does the **ar** sound in the word **Bart**?

Point to each sound as you say it.

B ar

CULTIVATING READING AND PHONICS SKILLS 1ST GRADE – 3RD GRADE

B**ar**   t

B**ar**t

And what is the *ar* going to sound like in this word **sharks**?

Point to each sound as you say it.

s   m

sm   **ar**

sm**ar**   t

sm**ar**t

Point to each sound as you say it.

sh   **ar**

sh**ar**   k

sh**ar**   s

sh**ar**ks

READ AND SPELL WORDS FROM THE STORY (10 TO 20 MINUTES)

MATERIALS – "Bart from Mars" in the book, *Phonics Stories: Long Vowels*, by Laurie Hunter; *the* student's 3-D Flash Cards; Dot stickers; Spotlighting penlight; and orange marker

AT THE BEGINNING OF EVERY SESSION – Review the student's 3-D Flash Cards.

READ THE STORY – As the student reads the story, use the 3-D Flash Cards, Dot Time, or Spotlighting to help the student figure out difficult words.

NOTE – If the student made three or more errors while reading the story, then have the student read the story once again to build word recognition and fluency. The student should reread and master each story before progressing to the next one.

INSTRUCTOR SAYS – For this activity, you will spell seven *ar* words from the story. **The purpose of this exercise is for you to say each word you spell so slowly that you can hear each sound as you write each letter.**

Spell ar Words from "Bart from Mars"
Bart
Mars
park
car
sharks
far
star
smart
art

DURING THIS ACTIVITY – Cover the spelling words, so your student can't see them. Provide immediate feedback for correct responses with stars or happy faces. More importantly, provide immediate feedback for all errors by writing the correct word with a yellow marker and **ask the student to trace over each letter while saying its corresponding sound**.

EXPLAIN – Look over all the words you spelled. Trace over the letters *ar* with orange marker. The /ar/ sounds like the name of the letter *r*, doesn't it?

NOTE for English language learners – English language learners should sketch a drawing next to each word they spell, unless it is a word they already know. Talk about the meaning of each word. Afterwards, ask the student to create one sentence using two of the words. Model writing the sentence for the student with your yellow marker. Then ask the student to trace the yellow words.

CULTIVATING READING AND PHONICS SKILLS 1ST GRADE – 3RD GRADE

Spell *The Other* Vowel Sounds from "Bart from Mars"

headline
armline
footline

a b c d e f g h i j k l m

n o p q r s t u v w x y z

IDENTIFY AND HIGHLIGHT *THE OTHER* VOWEL SOUNDS (10 MINUTES)

MATERIALS – "The Stork" passage below; yellow marker

INSTRUCTOR SAYS – Look at the passage below. Look inside each word and highlight with a yellow marker the **or**.

The Stork

A stork was born in a fort.
The stork lived in a fort and ate corn with a fork.

The stork was bored with corn and living in a fort.
The stork wanted more.

So, the stork rode his horse to the store to find more.
He was amazed when he walked in the door of the store.

But, shopping was a chore and a bore.
Shopping made his feet sore.

The stork no longer wanted more.
He went home to his fort and happily ate more corn.

EXPLAIN – Point to the word **stork** in the title of the story.

A stork is a long-legged bird with a large bill. What does the **or** sound like in the word **stork**?

Point to each sound as you say it.

s t **or**

  st**or** k

    st**or**k

CULTIVATING READING AND PHONICS SKILLS 1ST GRADE – 3RD GRADE

What does the *or* sound like in the word **born**?

Point to each sound as you say it.

b **or**

b**or** n

b**or**n

And what is the *or* going to sound like in this word **bore**? The **silent e** does not make the vowel say its name in the word **bore**. So the **o** will not say its name like it does in vowel teams. The **o** will not say its name in these words below either.

Point to each sound as you say the following words.

b **or** e (silent e)

m **or** e (silent e)

ch **or** e (silent e)

s t **or** e (silent e)

READ AND SPELL WORDS FROM THE STORY (10 TO 20 MINUTES)

MATERIALS – "The Stork" in the book, *Phonics Stories: Long Vowels,* by Laurie Hunter; *the* student's 3-D Flash Cards; Dot stickers; Spotlighting penlight; and **orange marker**

AT THE BEGINNING OF EVERY SESSION – Review the student's 3-D Flash Cards.

READ THE STORY – As the student reads the story, use the 3-D Flash Cards, Dot Time, or Spotlighting to help the student figure out difficult words.

NOTE – If the student made three or more errors while reading the story, then have the student read the story once again to build word recognition and fluency. The student should reread and master each story before progressing to the next one.

INSTRUCTOR SAYS – For this activity, I will select eight words with *or* from the story. **The purpose of this exercise is for you to say each word you spell so slowly that you can hear each sound as you write each letter.**

Spell or Words from "The Stork"	
stork	bore
born	bored
fort	more
corn	horse
fork	store
door	chore
	sore

DURING THIS ACTIVITY – Cover the spelling words, so your student can't see them. Provide immediate feedback for correct responses with stars or happy faces. More importantly, provide immediate feedback for all errors by writing the correct word with a yellow marker and **ask the student to trace over each letter while saying its corresponding sound**.

EXPLAIN – Look over all the words you spelled. Trace over the letters *or* make the /or/ sound with *orange* marker. The /or/ sound is spelled just like the word *or*. We use the word *or* every day, don't we? It's not only a word; *or* is also a letter group in many words.

NOTE for English language learners – English language learners should sketch a drawing next to each word they spell, unless it is a word they already know. Talk about the meaning of each word. Afterwards, ask the student to create one sentence using two of the words. Model writing the sentence for the student with your yellow marker. Then ask the student to trace the yellow words.

CULTIVATING READING AND PHONICS SKILLS 1ST GRADE – 3RD GRADE

Spell *The Other* Vowel Sounds from "The Stork"

headline
armline
footline

abcdefghijklm

nopqrstuvwxyz

IDENTIFY AND HIGHLIGHT THE OTHER VOWEL SOUNDS (10 MINUTES)

MATERIALS – "You Are Perfect" passage below; yellow marker

INSTRUCTOR SAYS – Look at the passage below. Look inside each word and highlight with a yellow marker the **er, ir,** and **ur**.

EXPLAIN – If you have a **vowel** plus the letter **r**, together they make a new sound. The **r** controls the vowel to change its sound. You learned that **ar** makes the /r/ sound in **star** and **Mars** and that the letter group **or** makes the sound in **fork** and **stork**.

What sound does the **er**, **ir**, and **ur** make in the words: **germ**, **shirt**, and **fur**?

They make the same sound, don't they? The **er**, **ir**, and **ur** sound the same, but **ar** and **or** sound different. Let's review, what sound does the **ar** make in the word **star**? What sound does the **or** make in **fork**? What sound do you hear in g**er**m, sh**ir**t, and f**ur**?

You Are Perfect!

A girl went to the nurse.
The girl went to the nurse because she was hurt.

The nurse asked, "How were you hurt?"

A girl in class had hurt her.
She made her feel like dirt.

The nurse said, "That girl had some nerve! You are not dirt! You are perfect."

When a person makes you feel like dirt, remember this:

It is not about you.
Something is hurting inside that person.
They burn and blurt words that hurt others.
It is not about you, it's about them.
They hurt and act like a jerk.

CULTIVATING READING AND PHONICS SKILLS 1ST GRADE – 3RD GRADE

 **EXPLAIN** – Point to the word **perfect** in the title of the story.

What is the **er** going to sound like in the word **perfect**?

Point to each sound as you say it.

p **er**

p**er** f

p**er**f e c t

And what is the **ur** going to sound like in this word **nurse** or **hurting**?

Point to each sound as you say it.

n **ur** s e (silent e)

h **ur** t ing

Point to each sound as you say the word **nerve**.

n **er** v e (silent e)

READ AND SPELL WORDS FROM THE STORY (10 TO 20 MINUTES)

 **MATERIALS** – "You Are Perfect" in the book, *Phonics Stories: Long Vowels,* by Laurie Hunter; *the* student's 3-D Flash Cards; Dot stickers; Spotlighting penlight; and orange marker

AT THE BEGINNING OF EVERY SESSION – Review the student's 3-D Flash Cards.

READ THE STORY – As the student reads the story, use the 3-D Flash Cards, Dot Time, or Spotlighting to help the student figure out difficult words.

 **NOTE** – If the student made three or more errors while reading the story, then have the student reread the story again to build word recognition and fluency. The student should reread and master each story before progressing to the next one.

INSTRUCTOR SAYS – For this activity, I will select eight **er, ir, and ur** words from the story. **The purpose of this exercise is for you to say each word you spell so slowly that you can hear each sound as you write each letter.**

Spell er, ir, and ur Words from "You Are Perfect"		
per-fect	girl	nurse
were (silent e)	dirt	hurt
her		hurt-ing
nerve		burn
per-son		blurt
jerk		

DURING THIS ACTIVITY – Cover the spelling words, so student can't see them. Provide immediate feedback for correct responses with stars or happy faces. More importantly, provide immediate feedback for all errors by writing the correct word with a yellow marker and **ask student to trace over each letter while saying its corresponding sound**.

EXPLAIN – Look over all the words you spelled. Trace over the letters *er*, *ir*, and *ur* with orange marker. The /er/ sound is spelled three different ways, but all three spellings make the same sound.

NOTE for English language learners – English language learners should sketch a drawing next to each word they spell, unless it is a word they already know. Talk about the meaning of each word. Afterwards, ask the student to create one sentence using two of the words. Model writing the sentence for the student with your yellow marker. Then ask the student to trace the yellow words.

CULTIVATING READING AND PHONICS SKILLS 1ST GRADE – 3RD GRADE

Spell *The Other* Vowel Sounds from "You Are Perfect"

headline
armline
footline

abcdefghijklm

nopqrstuvwxyz

IDENTIFY AND HIGHLIGHT *THE OTHER* VOWEL SOUNDS (10 MINUTES)

 **MATERIALS** – "Give Joy, Not Destroy" passage below; yellow marker

 **INSTRUCTOR SAYS** – Look at the passage below. Look inside each word and highlight with a yellow marker the *oy* and *oi*'s.

Give Joy, Not Destroy

The boy had a friend.
The boy's friend said, "Let's smoke a joint."

"I think smoke is poison."
His friend said, "It is not poison.
It will make you feel joy."

"But other things can give us joy.
I think smoke can destroy cells in our lungs and brain.
I think it's a bad choice."

His friend said, "Good point."

The voice in the boy's head said, "I want to make a better choices.
I'll spend my coins on toys that give joy."

 **EXPLAIN** – Point to the word *point* in the story.

What is the *oi* going to sound like in the word *point*?

Point to each sound as you say it.

p oi

 p**oi** n

  p**oi**n t

CULTIVATING READING AND PHONICS SKILLS 1ST GRADE – 3RD GRADE

And what is the **oy** going to sound like in this word **joy**?

Point to each sound as you say it.

j **oy**

Point to each sound as you say the word **destroy**.

d**e**

d**e** s t r

d**e** str **oy**

What does **destroy** mean? (to damage, ruin, or kill)

There are two ways we spell the /oy/ sound in English. Words like **point, joint**, and **poison** use **oi** and words like **joy, boy**, and **destroy** use **oy**.

Point to each sound as you say the word **voice**.

v **oi**

v**oi** **c**e

In this word, the letter **c** is followed by **silent e**. When **c** is followed by an **e**, **i**, or **y**, it makes the **cereal** /s/ sound. If **c** is followed by any other letter, it makes the **cat** sound.

Point to each sound as you say the word **choice**.

ch **oi**

ch**oi** **c**e

The **c** is followed by **silent e**, so it makes the **cereal** /s/ sound also.

READ AND SPELL WORDS FROM THE STORY (10 TO 20 MINUTES)

MATERIALS – "Give Joy, Not Destroy" in the book, *Phonics Stories: Long Vowels, by Laurie* Hunter; *the* student's 3-D Flash Cards; Spotlighting penlight; and **orange marker**

AT THE BEGINNING OF EVERY SESSION – Review the student's 3-D Flash Cards.

READ THE STORY – As the student reads the story, use the 3-D Flash Cards, Dot Time, or Spotlighting to help the student figure out difficult words.

NOTE – If the student made three or more errors while reading the story, then have the student read the story once again to build word recognition and fluency. The student should reread and master each story before progressing to the next one.

INSTRUCTOR SAYS – For this activity, I will select eight **oy** and **oi** words from the story. **The purpose of this exercise is for you to say each word you spell so slowly that you can hear each sound as you write each letter.**

Spell oy and oi Words from "Give Joy, Not Destroy"	
joy	joint
boy	poi-son
de-stroy	choice
toy	point
	voice
	coins

DURING THIS ACTIVITY – Cover the spelling words, so your student can't see them. Provide immediate feedback for correct responses with stars or happy faces. More importantly, provide immediate feedback for all errors by writing the correct word with a yellow marker and **ask the student to trace over each letter while saying its corresponding sound**.

EXPLAIN – Look over all the words you spelled. Trace over the letters *oy* and *oi* that make the /oy/ sound with orange marker. The /oy/ sound is spelled two different ways, but both spellings make the same sound.

NOTE for English language learners – English language learners should sketch a drawing next to each word they spell, unless it is a word they already know. Talk about the meaning of each word. Afterwards, ask the student to create one sentence using two of the words. Model writing the sentence for the student with your yellow marker. Then ask the student to trace the yellow words.

CULTIVATING READING AND PHONICS SKILLS 1ST GRADE – 3RD GRADE

Spell *The Other* Vowel Sounds from "Give Joy, Not Destroy"

headline
armline
footline

a b c d e f g h i j k l m

n o p q r s t u v w x y z

162

STEP 7 | TEACH ADVANCED LONG AND SHORT VOWEL PATTERNS

> *"Let us proudly be the crazy ones, the ambitious ones, the ones who see beyond the limits of today, who capture the opportunities, who find the resources that will build a better tomorrow, not for ourselves, but for those depending upon us to get it right."*
>
> Ertharin Cousin

MAKE 3-D FLASH CARDS FOR MORE LONG VOWEL SOUNDS

MATERIALS – Visuals for the keywords; 3-D Flash Cards for the **Advanced Long Vowel Spelling Patterns** (See Appendix B); colored markers that include a **blue marker**

INSTRUCTOR SAYS – Let's review. What are the vowels? (*a*, *e*, *i*, *o*, *u*, and sometimes *y*)

Every word and syllable must have a what? (a vowel)

What is a long vowel sound? (Say the name of a vowel and that is a long vowel sound.)

Look at each 3-D Flash Card to learn advanced ways we spell long vowel sounds. These combinations of letters must be memorized. The flash cards and the keywords will help you remember them.

CULTIVATING READING AND PHONICS SKILLS 1ST GRADE – 3RD GRADE

Advanced Long Vowel Spelling Patterns	Visual and Keyword
ie	cookie
y	baby
igh	night light
y	butterfly
ow	blowfish
ol	goldfish
ew	stew
oo	moon

EXPLAIN – The letter group *ie* and *y* can both make the **long e** sound. Do you hear the long e sound on the end of the words, **cookie** and **baby**? But **cookie** is spelled with *ie* and **baby** ends with the letter *y*.

The letter *y* at the end of a word can make a **long e** sound or a **long i** sound. Do you hear the **long e** sound in the words **happy, funny, bunny, lucky,** and **candy**?

Do you hear the **long i** sound in the words **fly, try, cry, my,** and **by**?

We'll learn the advanced spelling patterns with each story we read.

164

3-D Flash Cards: **Advanced Long Vowel Spelling Patterns: ie y igh y ow ol ew oo**
Student colors letter groups with a **blue marker** then draws the keyword for each card.

165

CULTIVATING READING AND PHONICS SKILLS 1ST GRADE – 3RD GRADE

3-D Flash Cards: Advanced Long Vowel Spelling Patterns: ie y igh y ow ol ew oo
Student color groups letters with a **blue marker** then draws the keyword for each card.

166

LAURIE HUNTER

IDENTIFY AND HIGHLIGHT THE LONG VOWEL SOUNDS (10 MINUTES)

MATERIALS – "The Field Trip" passage below; yellow marker

INSTRUCTOR SAYS – Look at the passage below. Look inside each word and highlight with a yellow marker the **long e** sounds (*ie* and *y*) on this worksheet.

The Field Trip

My niece is a happy baby.
My niece is a happy baby with curly hair.
She has curly hair and a pretty smile.

My niece and I went on a field trip to a bakery.
At the bakery, we learned how to make cookies and candy.

After the field trip, my niece and I saw a funny movie.
We ate cookies and candy at the movie.
It was a fun day with my niece!

EXPLAIN – Look at the **long e** sounds (*ie* and *y*) you highlighted with yellow marker. The *ie* and *y* can make the **long e** sound.

Point to the word **field** in the title of the story.

A field trip is a trip people take to learn or study something firsthand. What is the *ie* going to sound like in the word **field**?

Point to each sound as you say it.

f **ie** l d

What is the *ie* going to sound like in the word **niece**?

Point to each sound as you say it.

n **ie** ce (silent e)

167

CULTIVATING READING AND PHONICS SKILLS 1ST GRADE – 3RD GRADE

The **c** is followed by **silent e**, so it makes the **cereal** /s/ sound.

What is a **niece**? A niece is the daughter of one's brother or sister. So, if you have a sister or brother, and they have a daughter, she would be your niece.

The letter **y** can make the **long e** sound like you hear on the end of words like **happy** and **baby**.

Point to each sound as you say **happy**.

h a p

hap py

happy

Point to each sound as you say **curly**.

c ur

cur l

curl y

curly

Point to each sound as you say **baby**.

ba

ba by

Point to each sound as you say **bakery**.

ba

ba ker

baker y

READ AND SPELL WORDS FROM THE STORY (10 TO 20 MINUTES)

MATERIALS – "The Field Trip" in the book, *Phonics Stories: Advanced Long and Short Vowel Patterns* by Laurie Hunter; the student's 3-D Flash Cards; Dot Time stickers; Spotlighting penlight; yellow marker; **blue marker**

AT THE BEGINNING OF EVERY SESSION – Review the student's 3-D Flash Cards.

READ THE STORY – As the student reads the story, use the 3-D Flash Cards, Dot Time, or Spotlighting to help the student figure out difficult words.

NOTE – If the student made three or more errors while reading the story, then have the student read the story once again to build word recognition and fluency. The student should reread and master each story before progressing to the next one.

INSTRUCTOR SAYS – For this activity, I will select eight *ie* and *y* words from the story. **The purpose of this exercise is for you to say each word you spell so slowly that you can hear each sound as you write each letter.**

Spell ie and y Words from "The Field Trip"	
niece	hap-py
field	ba-by
cook-ie	cur-ly
cook-ies	pret-ty
mov-ie	ba-ker-y
can-dies	can-dy
	fun-ny

DURING THIS ACTIVITY – Cover the spelling words, so your student can't see them. Provide immediate feedback for correct responses with stars or happy faces. More importantly, provide immediate feedback for all errors by writing the correct word with a yellow marker and **ask the student to trace over each letter while saying its corresponding sound.**

EXPLAIN – Look over all the words you spelled. Trace over the letters *ie* and *y*.

So far, we've learned five ways we can spell the **long e** sound in English.

CULTIVATING READING AND PHONICS SKILLS 1ST GRADE – 3RD GRADE

1) One way is when **e** is at the end of a word or syllable, the vowel says its name.

m**e**

m**e**t**e**or (**me-te-or**)

2) Another is when two vowels hold hands in the vowel teams **ea, ee**, and **ey**, the first vowel says its name.

b**ea**ds

tr**ee**

k**ey**

3) When a vowel and **silent e** are jumping rope with a consonant, the first vowel will say its name.

g**e**n**e**

4) An advanced way to spell the **long e** sound is the letter group **ie**.

cook**ie**

5) Another advanced **long e** spelling pattern is the letter **y**.

bab**y**

 **NOTE for English language learners** – English language learners should sketch a drawing next to each word they spell, unless it is a word they already know. Talk about the meaning of each word. Afterwards, ask the student to create one sentence using two of the words. Model writing the sentence for the student with your yellow marker. Then ask the student to trace the yellow words.

Spell Advanced Long e Spelling Patterns from "The Field Trip"

headline
armline
footline

a b c d e f g h i j k l m
n o p q r s t u v w x y z

CULTIVATING READING AND PHONICS SKILLS 1ST GRADE – 3RD GRADE

IDENTIFY AND HIGHLIGHT THE LONG VOWEL SOUNDS (10 MINUTES)

MATERIALS – "Just Try" passage below; yellow marker

INSTRUCTOR SAYS – Look at the passage below. Look inside each word and highlight with a yellow marker the **long i** sounds (*i* on the end of words and syllables, *i_e*, and **y**).

Just Try

I saw the fly cry.
I saw the fly cry, and I asked why.
"Why are you crying?"

The fly said he did not know why he was crying.
I said there must be a reason why.
The fly said the reason why is because he could not fly in the sky.

I asked him to dry his tears.
I asked him to dry his tears and try to fly again.

Oh my! He did fly in the sky.
He did not cry.
He thanked me for asking him to dry his tears and try to fly again.

EXPLAIN – Look at the **long i** sounds you highlighted with yellow marker. Point to the word **try** in the title of the story.

What does the **y** sound like in this word?

The **y** says, "*i*." Isn't *i* the name of a vowel?

What is the **y** going to sound like in the word **fly**?

What is the **y** going to sound like in the word **cry**ing (POINT TO)?

Point to each sound as you say it.

wh **y**

t r **y**

c r **y**

cr**y** ing

READ AND SPELL WORDS FROM THE STORY (10 TO 20 MINUTES)

 **MATERIALS** – "Just Try" in the book, *Phonics Stories: Advanced Long and Short Vowel Patterns,* by Laurie Hunter; the student's 3-D Flash Cards; Dot Time stickers; Spotlighting penlight; yellow marker; **blue marker**

AT THE BEGINNING OF EVERY SESSION – Review the student's 3-D Flash Cards.

READ THE STORY – As the student reads the story, use the 3-D Flash Cards, Dot Time, or Spotlighting to help the student figure out difficult words.

 **NOTE** – If the student made three or more errors while reading the story, then have the student read the story once again to build word recognition and fluency. The student should reread and master each story before progressing to the next one.

 **INSTRUCTOR SAYS** – For this activity, I will select eight **y** words from the story. **The purpose of this exercise is for you to say each word you spell so slowly that you can hear each sound as you write each letter.**

Spell y Words from "Just Try"
fly
cry
cry-ing
why
sky
dry
try
my

CULTIVATING READING AND PHONICS SKILLS 1ST GRADE – 3RD GRADE

DURING THIS ACTIVITY – Cover the spelling words, so your student can't see them. Provide immediate feedback for correct responses with stars or happy faces. More importantly, provide immediate feedback for all errors by writing the correct word with a yellow marker and **ask the student to trace over each letter while saying its corresponding sound**.

EXPLAIN – Now look over all the words you spelled and trace over the letters (**y**) that make the **long i** sound with **blue marker**.

NOTE for English language learners – English language learners should sketch a drawing next to each word they spell, unless it is a word they already know. Talk about the meaning of each word. Afterwards, ask the student to create one sentence using two of the words. Model writing the sentence for the student with your yellow marker. Then ask the student to trace the yellow words.

Spell Advanced Long i Spelling Patterns from "Just Try"

headline
armline
footline

a b c d e f g h i j k l m

n o p q r s t u v w x y z

CULTIVATING READING AND PHONICS SKILLS 1ST GRADE – 3RD GRADE

IDENTIFY AND HIGHLIGHT THE LONG VOWEL SOUNDS (10 MINUTES)

 **MATERIALS** – "The Brave Knight, the Bright Fair Maid" passage below; yellow marker

 **INSTRUCTOR SAYS** – Look at the passage below. Look inside each word and highlight with a yellow marker the **long i** sounds (*-i, i_e, igh,* and *y*) on this worksheet.

The Brave Knight and the Bright Fair Maid

A knight saw a dragon.
The knight saw a dragon high in a cave.
The dragon breathed fire.
He breathed fire that could light up the darkest night!

A maid yelled, "Help!" from inside the cave.
The brave knight said, "Dragon, release her or I shall fight you!"

The dragon said, "I am not frightened of you.
Try to fight me with all your might."
As the dragon breathed fire, he did not see the fair maid run out of the cave!

The brave knight and the fair maid raced back to the castle.

The maid asked the knight, "Are you all right?"

The knight said, "Well, I was frightened. But it is important to fight for what is right. Lucky for me, you were bright. You ran, so I did not have to fight for what was right!"

 **EXPLAIN** – Look at the **long i** sounds (*igh* and *y*) you highlighted with yellow marker. The *igh* and *y* make the **long i** sound.

Point to the word **knight** in the title of the story. What is a **knight**? A long time ago knights would protect and defend a king, queen, or someone who owned a lot of land.

What is the **igh** going to sound like in the word **knight**?

Point to each sound as you say it.

k n **igh** t

The **k** in the word **knight** is silent. **K** is silent in some other words like **knee** and **knife**.

The **igh** is pronounced with a **long i** sound.

Point to each sound as you say it.

s **igh** t

b r **igh** t

f r **igh** t

    fr**igh**t e n

        fr**igh**ten ed

Remember **-d** and **-ed** on the end of words can be pronounced /ed/ or /d/. Here it is pronounced /d/.

READ AND SPELL WORDS FROM THE STORY (10 TO 20 MINUTES)

MATERIALS – "The Brave Knight" in *Phonics Stories: Advanced Long and Short Vowel Patterns* by Laurie Hunter; the student's 3-D Flash Cards; Dot Time stickers; Spotlighting penlight; yellow marker; **blue marker**

AT THE BEGINNING OF EVERY SESSION – Review the student's 3-D Flash Cards.

READ THE STORY – As the student reads the story, use the 3-D Flash Cards, Dot Time, or Spotlighting to help the student figure out difficult words.

NOTE – If the student made three or more errors while reading the story, then have the student read the story once again to build word recognition and fluency. The student should reread and master each story before progressing to the next one.

INSTRUCTOR SAYS – For this activity, I will select eight **igh** words from the story. **The purpose of this exercise is for you to say each word you spell so slowly that you can hear each sound as you write each letter.**

CULTIVATING READING AND PHONICS SKILLS 1ST GRADE – 3RD GRADE

Spell ight Words from "The Brave Knight…"
knight
bright
light
night
high
fight
fright
might
right

DURING THIS ACTIVITY – Cover the spelling words, so your student can't see them. Provide immediate feedback for correct responses with stars or happy faces. More importantly, provide immediate feedback for all errors by writing the correct word with a yellow marker and **ask the student to trace over each letter while saying its corresponding sound.**

EXPLAIN – Now look over all the words you spelled and trace over the letters (**igh** and **y**) that make the **long i** sound with **blue marker**.

We've learned five ways we can spell the **long i** sound in English.

1) One way is when the vowel **i** is at the end of a word or syllable, the vowel says its name.

h**i**

t**i** ger

2) Another is when two vowels hold hands in the vowel team **ie**, the first vowel says its name.

p**ie**

3) When a vowel and **silent e** are jumping rope with a consonant, the first vowel will say its name.

b**i**k**e**

178

4) An advanced way to spell the **long i** sound is the letter **y**.

*fl**y***

butt**erfl**y

5) Another advanced **long i** spelling pattern is the letter group **igh**.

*n**igh**t l**igh**t*

NOTE for English language learners – English language learners should sketch a drawing next to each word they spell, unless it is a word they already know. Talk about the meaning of each word. Afterwards, ask the student to create one sentence using two of the words. Model writing the sentence for the student with your yellow marker. Then ask the student to trace the yellow words.

CULTIVATING READING AND PHONICS SKILLS 1ST GRADE – 3RD GRADE

Spell Advanced Long i Spelling Patterns from "The Brave Knight and the Bright Maid"

headline
armline
footline

abcdefghijklm

nopqrstuvwxyz

IDENTIFY AND HIGHLIGHT THE LONG VOWEL SOUNDS (10 MINUTES)

MATERIALS – "The Teenage Blowfish and the Old Goldfish" passage below; yellow marker

INSTRUCTOR SAYS – Look at the passage below. Look inside each word and highlight with a yellow marker the **long o** sounds (**-o**, **ow**, and **ol**) on this worksheet.

The Teen Blowfish and the Old Goldfish

The old goldfish asked the teen blowfish, "What do you want to be when you grow up?"

The teen told the goldfish, "I don't know.
When I grow up, I think I will just go with the flow."

The old fish said, "If you go with the flow, that is like throwing away gold.
I am a goldfish. I don't want you to throw away gold!"

The old fish said, "Dear young blowfish, how would you like your life to be when you are older?"

The teen blowfish said, "I want to be a better student."

"If you want to be a better student, then sow seeds that will make you grow."

Dear Reader, how would you like your life to be when you are older?
What "seeds" can you sow?

EXPLAIN – Point to the word **blowfish** in the title of the story.

What is the **ow** going to sound like in the word **blowfish**?

Point to each sound as you say it.

CULTIVATING READING AND PHONICS SKILLS 1ST GRADE – 3RD GRADE

b l **ow**

   bl**ow** f i sh

      bl**ow**fish

What is the **ow** going to sound like in the word **grow**?

g r **ow**

th r **ow**

Point to the word **old** in the title of the story.

What is the **ol** going to sound like in the word **old** and **goldfish**?

Point to each sound as you say it.

ol d

g **ol** d

   g**ol**d f i sh

      g**ol**dfish

READ AND SPELL WORDS FROM THE STORY (10 TO 20 MINUTES)

MATERIALS – "The Teenage Blowfish and the Old Goldfish" in the book, *Phonics Stories: Advanced Long and Short Vowel Patterns* by Laurie Hunter; the student's 3-D Flash Cards; Dot Time stickers; Spotlighting penlight; yellow marker; **blue marker**

AT THE BEGINNING OF EVERY SESSION – Review the student's 3-D Flash Cards.

READ THE STORY – As the student reads the story, use the 3-D Flash Cards, Dot Time, or Spotlighting to help the student figure out difficult words.

NOTE – If the student made three or more errors while reading the story, then have the student read the story once again to build word recognition and fluency. The student should reread and master each story before progressing to the next one.

 **INSTRUCTOR SAYS** – For this activity, I will select eight *ol* and *ow* words from the story for you to spell. **The purpose of this exercise is for you to say each word you spell so slowly that you can hear each sound as you write each letter.**

Spell ol and ow Words from "The Teen Blowfish and the Old Goldfish"	
old	blow
old-er	grow
told	know
gold	flow
	throw
	throw-ing
	sow

DURING THIS ACTIVITY – Cover the spelling words, so your student can't see them. Provide immediate feedback for correct responses with stars or happy faces. More importantly, provide immediate feedback for all errors by writing the correct word with a yellow marker and **ask the student to trace over each letter while saying its corresponding sound**.

 **EXPLAIN** – Look over all the words you spelled. Trace over the letters **ow** and **ol** that make the **long o** sound with blue marker.

We've learned five ways we can spell the **long o** sound in English.

1) One way is when the vowel **o** is at the end of a word or syllable the vowel says its name.

n**o**

p**ho**to (p**ho**-to)

2) Another is when two vowels hold hands in the vowel team **oa**, the first vowel says its name.

b**oa**t

3) Also, when a vowel and **silent e** are jumping rope, the first vowel will say its name.

h**ole**

CULTIVATING READING AND PHONICS SKILLS 1ST GRADE – 3RD GRADE

4) The letter group **ow**

bl*ow*fish

5) The letter group **ol**

g*ol*dfish

NOTE for English language learners – English language learners should sketch a drawing next to each word they spell, unless it is a word they already know. Talk about the meaning of each word. Afterwards, ask the student to create one sentence using two of the words. Model writing the sentence for the student with your yellow marker. Then ask the student to trace the yellow words.

Spell Advanced Long o Spelling Pattern from "The Teen Blowfish and the Old Goldfish"

abcdefghijklm
nopqrstuvwxyz

CULTIVATING READING AND PHONICS SKILLS 1ST GRADE – 3RD GRADE

IDENTIFY AND HIGHLIGHT THE LONG VOWEL SOUNDS (10 MINUTES)

 **MATERIALS** – "The Baboon, His Loose Tooth, and the Kangaroo" passage below; yellow marker

 **INSTRUCTOR SAYS** – Look at the passage below. Look inside each word and highlight with a yellow marker the **long u** sounds (**oo**) on this worksheet.

The Baboon, His Loose Tooth, and the Kangaroo

It was noon at the zoo and the baboon was moody.
He had a loose tooth and could not chew any food.
"Boohoo!" cried the moody baboon.
"My tooth hurts!"

The kangaroo said to the baboon, "I know just what to do!"
He said, "It will hurt, but I will pull out your loose tooth."

He reached into his pouch for his loose tooth tool.
With his handy tool, the kangaroo yanked out the baboon's loose tooth.

The baboon cried a few big tears.
But soon, the hurt stopped, and he was no longer gloomy.

The baboon thanked the kangaroo because now he could chew his food!

 **EXPLAIN** – Point to the word **loose** in the title of the story.

What is the **oo** going to sound like in the word **loose**?

Point to each sound as you say it.

l oo

loo se

The **silent e** on the end of the word **loose** is silent and doesn't say anything.

Point to each sound as you say the word **baboon**.

b a b

  bab oo

    bab**oo** n

      bab**oo**n

Point to the sounds in the word **gloomy**?

g l

  gl oo

    gl**oo** m

      gl**oo**m y

READ AND SPELL WORDS FROM THE STORY (10 TO 20 MINUTES)

MATERIALS – "The Baboon, His Loose Tooth, and the Kangaroo" in the book, *Phonics Stories: Advanced Long and Short Vowel Patterns* by Laurie Hunter; the student's 3-D Flash Cards; Dot Time stickers; Spotlighting penlight; yellow marker; **blue marker**

AT THE BEGINNING OF EVERY SESSION – Review the student's 3-D Flash Cards.

READ THE STORY – As the student reads the story, use the 3-D Flash Cards, Dot Time, or Spotlighting to help the student figure out difficult words.

NOTE – If the student made three or more errors while reading the story, then have the student read the story once again to build word recognition and fluency. The student should reread and master each story before progressing to the next one.

INSTRUCTOR SAYS – For this activity, I will select eight **oo and o** words from the story. **The purpose of this exercise is for you to say each word you spell so slowly that you can hear each sound as you write each letter.**

CULTIVATING READING AND PHONICS SKILLS 1ST GRADE – 3RD GRADE

Spell oo Words from "The Baboon, His Loose Tooth, and the Kangaroo"		
bab-oon	chew	do
loose	few	to
tooth		into
kan-ga-roo		
noon		
zoo		
mood-y		
food		
boo-hoo		
tool		
soon		
gloom-y		

DURING THIS ACTIVITY – Cover the spelling words, so your student can't see them. Provide immediate feedback for correct responses with stars or happy faces. More importantly, provide immediate feedback for all errors by writing the correct word with a yellow marker and **ask the student to trace over each letter while saying its corresponding sound**.

EXPLAIN – Look over all the words you spelled. Trace over the letters **oo** and **o** that make the /oo/ sound with **blue** marker. The long u makes two sounds.

NOTE for English language learners – English language learners should sketch a drawing next to each word they spell, unless it is a word they already know. Talk about the meaning of each word. Afterwards, ask the student to create one sentence using two of the words. Model writing the sentence for the student with your yellow marker. Then ask the student to trace the yellow words.

LAURIE HUNTER

Spell Advanced Long u Spelling Patterns from "The Baboon, His Loose Tooth, and Kangaroo"

headline
armline
footline

a b c d e f g h i j k l m
n o p q r s t u v w x y z

MAKE 3-D FLASH CARDS FOR ADVANCED SHORT VOWEL SPELLING PATTERNS

MATERIALS – Visuals for the keywords; 3-D Flash Cards for the **Advanced Short Vowel Spelling Patterns** (See Appendix B); colored markers that include a **pink marker**

INSTRUCTOR SAYS – Let's review the short vowel sounds and their keywords.

The short vowel sounds are:

/a/ as in **a**pple

/e/ as in **e**lephant

/i/ as in **i**gloo

/o/ as in **o**ctopus

/u/ as in **u**mbrella

There are more advanced ways we can make short vowel sounds. These combinations of letters must be memorized. The 3-D Flash Cards and the keywords will help you remember them.

Advanced Short Vowel Spelling Patterns	Visual and Keyword
a (sounds like the u in **u**mbrella)	pand**a**
a (sounds like the o in **o**ctopus)	sp**a**
au (sounds like the o in **o**ctopus)	l**au**ndry
aw (sounds like the o in **o**ctopus)	str**aw**
al (sounds like the u in **o**ctopus + l)	ch**al**k
ea (sounds like the e in **e**lephant)	f**ea**ther
y (sounds like the i in **i**gloo)	g**y**m
o (sounds like the u in **u**mbrella)	l**o**ve

EXPLAIN – We'll learn the advanced spelling patterns with each story we read.

3-D Flash Cards: **Advanced Short Vowel Spelling Patterns: a a au aw al ea o y**
Student colors letter groups with **pink marker** then draws the keyword for each card.

CULTIVATING READING AND PHONICS SKILLS 1ST GRADE – 3RD GRADE

3-D Flash Cards: **Advanced Short Vowel Spelling Patterns: a a au aw al ea o y**
Student colors letters with **pink marker** then draws the keyword for each letter (group).

IDENTIFY AND HIGHLIGHT THE LONG VOWEL SOUNDS (10 MINUTES)

MATERIALS – "The Hawk and the Fawn" passage below; yellow marker

INSTRUCTOR SAYS – Look at the passage below. Look inside each word and highlight with a yellow marker the letter groups **au, aw,** and **al** that make the **short o** sound.

The Hawk and the Fawn

The hawk was sitting in a tree.
The hawk in the tree saw a fawn on the lawn.

The fawn saw the hawk.
The fawn asked the hawk to play ball.

The hawk said, "I'd love to play ball. But, I can't because my short legs cannot kick a ball."

The fawn asked, "Would you like to draw?"

The hawk said, "I can't because my wings cannot hold a pencil to draw. Would you like to fly with me?"

The fawn said, "I can jump.
But I cannot fly because I do not have wings.
But these differences are not faults.
We don't have to play ball, draw, or fly to have fun.
We can talk!"
Let's talk!"

 **EXPLAIN** – Point to the word **hawk** in the title of the story.

A hawk is a type of a bird. What does the **aw** sound like in the word **hawk**? (/o/ like in the word **o**ctopus)

Point to each sound as you say it.

h **aw**   (the **aw** sounds like the o in **o**ctopus)

h**aw** k

h**aw**k

What does the **aw** sound like in the word **fawn**? (/o/ like in the word **o**ctopus)

A fawn is a young deer. Point to each sound as you say it.

f **aw**

CULTIVATING READING AND PHONICS SKILLS 1ST GRADE – 3RD GRADE

f aw n

fawn

Say these words as you point to each sound.

d r aw

draw

b al   (the **al** sounds like the o in **octopus** + **l**)

ball

READ AND SPELL WORDS FROM THE STORY (10 TO 20 MINUTES)

MATERIALS – "The Hawk and the Fawn" in the book, *Phonics Stories: Advanced Long and Short Vowel Patterns* by Laurie Hunter; the student's 3-D Flash Cards; Dot Time stickers; Spotlighting penlight; yellow marker; **pink marker**

AT THE BEGINNING OF EVERY SESSION – Review the student's 3-D Flash Cards.

READ THE STORY – As the student reads the story, use the 3-D Flash Cards, Dot Time, or Spotlighting to help the student figure out difficult words.

NOTE – If the student made three or more errors while reading the story, then have the student read the story once again to build word recognition and fluency. The student should reread and master each story before progressing to the next one.

INSTRUCTOR SAYS – For this activity, you will spell eight **aw**, **au**, and **al** words from the story. **The purpose of this exercise is for you to say each word you spell so slowly that you can hear each sound as you write each letter.**

Spel Advancedl Short o Words from "The Hawk and the Fawn"		
hawk	be-cause	ball
fawn	faults	talk
saw		
lawn		
draw		

DURING THIS ACTIVITY – Cover the spelling words, so your student can't see them. Provide immediate feedback for correct responses with stars or happy faces. More importantly, provide immediate feedback for all errors by writing the correct word with a yellow marker and **ask the student to trace over each letter while saying its corresponding sound**.

EXPLAIN – Look over all the words you spelled and trace over the letters *aw, au,* and *al* that make the **short o** sound with pink marker.

The first Flash Card we made for the letter **o** was for the keyword *octopus*. We learned that when the letter **o** is not on the end of a word or syllable, **o** makes the **short o** vowel sound. The second **o** in *octopus* is at the end of a syllable, so it will make the **long o** sound and say its name.

oc-to-pus

In the English language, the letter groups *aw*, *au*, and *al* also make the **short o** vowel sound.

straw

laundry

chalk

NOTE for English language learners – English language learners should sketch a drawing next to each word they spell, unless it is a word they already know. Talk about the meaning of each word. Afterwards, ask the student to create one sentence using two of the words. Model writing the sentence for the student with your yellow marker. Then ask the student to trace the yellow words.

CULTIVATING READING AND PHONICS SKILLS 1ST GRADE – 3RD GRADE

Spell Advanced Short o Spelling Patterns from "The Hawk and the Fawn"

headline
armline
footline

abcdefghijklm

nopqrstuvwxyz

IDENTIFY AND HIGHLIGHT THE LONG VOWEL SOUNDS (10 MINUTES)

MATERIALS – "Mama Panda" passage below; yellow marker

INSTRUCTOR SAYS – Look at the passage below. Look inside each word and highlight with a yellow marker the letter ***a***'s that make the **short o** (**o**ctopus) sound and the **short u** (**u**mbrella) sound. Be careful! This passage has some ***a***'s that will make **apple** sound.

Mama Panda

The mama panda went to a spa.
The mama panda went to the spa so she could rest.

After she rested at the spa, she ate green pasta with a cup of water.
What a treat!

She said, "Ha ha! I like the spa and green pasta."
The mama panda felt rested and was happy.

EXPLAIN – Point to the word ***spa*** in the title of the story.

A spa is a place some people go to relax and receive health and beauty treatments. What does the ***a*** sound like in the word ***spa***? (/o/ like in the word ***octopus***)

Point to each sound as you say it.

s p a   (the a sounds like the o in **o**ctopus)

   spa

What do the ***a***'s sound like in the word ***mama***? (The first ***a*** sounds like /o/ like in the word ***octopus***. The second ***a*** sounds like the u in ***u**mbrella*.)

Mama is another name for a mother. Point to each sound as you say it.

CULTIVATING READING AND PHONICS SKILLS 1ST GRADE – 3RD GRADE

m a (the first **a** sounds like the o in **o**ctopus)

ma ma (the second **a** sounds like the u in **u**mbrella)

mama

Say these words as you point to each sound in the word **panda**.

p a n (the first **a** sounds like the a in **a**pple)

pan da (the second **a** sounds like the u in **u**mbrella)

panda

READ AND SPELL WORDS FROM THE STORY (10 TO 20 MINUTES)

MATERIALS – "Mama Panda" in the book, *Phonics Stories: Advanced Long and Short Vowel Patterns* by Laurie Hunter; the student's 3-D Flash Cards; Dot Time stickers; Spotlighting penlight; yellow marker; **pink marker**

AT THE BEGINNING OF EVERY SESSION – Review the student's 3-D Flash Cards.

READ THE STORY – As the student reads the story, use the 3-D Flash Cards, Dot Time, or Spotlighting to help the student figure out difficult words.

NOTE – If the student made more than three errors while reading the story, ask the student to read the story again to build word recognition and fluency. The student should master each story before progressing to the next one.

INSTRUCTOR SAYS – For this activity, you will spell five words from the story. **The purpose of this exercise is for you to say each word you spell so slowly that you can hear each sound as you write each letter or letter group.**

Spell Advanced Short u, Short o, and Short a Words from "Mama Panda"		
pan-da	spa	pan-da
ma-ma	ma-ma	at
pa-sta	pa-sta	af-ter
was	wa-ter	hap-py
what	ha ha!	

DURING THIS ACTIVITY – Cover the spelling words, so your student can't see them. Provide immediate feedback for correct responses with stars or happy faces. More importantly, provide immediate feedback for all errors by writing the correct word with a yellow marker and **ask the student to trace over each letter while saying its corresponding sound**.

EXPLAIN – Look over all the words you spelled and trace over the letters **aw, au,** and **al** that make the **short o** sound with pink marker.

We've learned four ways we can spell the **short o** sound in English. Let's review.

1) When the letter **o** is not on the end of a word or syllable

oc-to-pus

2) The letter group **aw**

straw

3) The letter group **au**

laundry

4) The letter group **al**

chalk

5) Another way to make **short o** sound is when **a** is at the end of a word or syllable.

spa

ha ha

NOTE for English language learners – English language learners should sketch a drawing next to each word they spell, unless it is a word they already know. Talk about the meaning of each word. Afterwards, ask the student to create one sentence using two of the words. Model writing the sentence for the student with your yellow marker. Then ask the student to trace the yellow words.

CULTIVATING READING AND PHONICS SKILLS 1ST GRADE – 3RD GRADE

Spell Advanced Short u, Short a, Short a Spelling Patterns from "Mama Panda"

abcdefghijklm
nopqrstuvwxyz

LAURIE HUNTER

IDENTIFY AND HIGHLIGHT THE LONG VOWEL SOUNDS (10 MINUTES)

 **MATERIALS** – "Jeff's Homemade Bread" passage below; yellow marker

 **INSTRUCTOR SAYS** – Look at the passage below. Look inside each word and highlight with a yellow marker the letter group **ea** that makes the **short e** sound.

Jeff's Homemade Bread

The bread was ready!
And, Jeff was ready to take the bread out of the oven.

The bread was hot and heavy.
Jeff's hot and heavy bread made him sweat.
He felt the sweat drip from his head.

Jeff took a deep breath.
The hot and heavy bread made him sweat.
Jeff took a deep breath to smell the bread.
It smelled so good!

Jeff spread butter on his bread.
He took a bite.
The bread was so good, Jeff thought he was dead and had gone to heaven!
"I'm in heaven!"

 **EXPLAIN** – Point to the word **bread** in the title of the story.

What does the **ea** sound like in the word **bread**? (/e/ like in the word **e**l**ephant**) Point to each sound as you say it.

b r **ea**   (the **ea** sounds like the e in **e**l**ephant**)

   br**ea** d

     br**ea**d

CULTIVATING READING AND PHONICS SKILLS 1ST GRADE – 3RD GRADE

What does the **ea** sound like in the word **heavy**? (/e/ like in the word **elephant**)

Point to each sound as you say it.

h **ea**

   h**ea** v

      h**ea**v y

         h**ea**v y

Say these words as you point to each sound.

b r **ea**

   br**ea**

      br**ea** th

         br**ea**th

READ AND SPELL WORDS FROM THE STORY (10 TO 20 MINUTES)

MATERIALS – "Jeff's Homemade Bread" in the book, *Phonics Stories: Long Vowel Patterns, by Laurie* Hunter; *the* student's 3-D Flash Cards; Dot stickers; Spotlighting penlight; **pink marker**.

AT THE BEGINNING OF EVERY SESSION – Review the student's 3-D Flash Cards.

READ THE STORY – As the student reads the story, use the 3-D Flash Cards, Dot Time, or Spotlighting to help the student figure out difficult words.

NOTE – If the student made three or more errors while reading the story, then have the student read the story once again to build word recognition and fluency. The student should reread and master each story before progressing to the next one.

INSTRUCTOR SAYS – For this activity, I will select eight **ea** words from the story. **The purpose of this exercise is for you to say each word you spell so slowly that you can hear each sound as you write each letter.**

Spell Advanced Short e Words from "Jeff's Homemade Bread"	
bread	Jeff
read-y	Jeff's
heav-y	ov-en
sweat	felt
head	smell
breath	smelled
spread	heav-en
dead	
heav-en	

DURING THIS ACTIVITY – Cover the spelling words, so your student can't see them. Provide immediate feedback for correct responses with stars or happy faces. More importantly, provide immediate feedback for all errors by writing the correct word with a yellow marker and **ask the student to trace over each letter while saying its corresponding sound**.

EXPLAIN – Look over all the words you spelled and trace over the letters *ea* that make the **short e** sound with pink marker.

We've learned two ways we can spell the **short e** sound in English.

1) When the letter **e** is not on the end of a word or syllable

elephant

2) The letter group **ea**

bread

NOTE for English language learners – English language learners should sketch a drawing next to each word they spell, unless it is a word they already know. Talk about the meaning of each word. Afterwards, ask the student to create one sentence using two of the words. Model writing the sentence for the student with your yellow marker. Then ask the student to trace the yellow words.

CULTIVATING READING AND PHONICS SKILLS 1ST GRADE – 3RD GRADE

Spell Advanced Short e Spelling Patterns from "Jeff's Homemade Bread"

headline
armline
footline

a b c d e f g h i j k l m

n o p q r s t u v w x y z

IDENTIFY AND HIGHLIGHT THE LONG VOWEL SOUNDS (10 MINUTES)

 **MATERIALS** – "Love" passage below; yellow marker

 **INSTRUCTOR SAYS** – Look at the passage below. Look inside each word and highlight with a yellow marker the letter **o**'s that makes the **short u** sound.

Love

The son was young.
The young son misses his mother and dad.
He wonders about his mother and dad.

He does not have a brother or sister.
He was raised by his grandmother.
His grandmother loves him a ton.
She smothers him with love.
She is wonderful!
There is no other who loves him as much as his grandmother.
No one.

"She loves me so much!"

EXPLAIN – Point to the word *love* in the title of the story.

What does the **o** sound like in the word **love**? (/u/ like in the word **u**mbrella)

Point to each sound as you say it.

l **o**   (the **o** sounds like the u in **u**mbrella)

l **o** ve   (silent e)

l **o**ve   s

l **o**ves

CULTIVATING READING AND PHONICS SKILLS 1ST GRADE – 3RD GRADE

Say these words as you point to each sound.

s o n

t o n

s o n

What does the **o** sound like in the word **mother**? (/u/ like in the word **umbrella**)

Point to each sound as you say it.

m o

mo th

moth er

mother

READ AND SPELL WORDS FROM THE STORY (10 TO 20 MINUTES)

MATERIALS – "Love" in the book, *Phonics Stories: Advanced Long and Short Vowel Patterns* by Laurie Hunter; the student's 3-D Flash Cards; Dot Time stickers; Spotlighting penlight; yellow marker; **pink marker**.

AT THE BEGINNING OF EVERY SESSION – Review the student's 3-D Flash Cards.

READ THE STORY – As the student reads the story, use the 3-D Flash Cards, Dot Time, or Spotlighting to help the student figure out difficult words.

NOTE – If the student made three or more errors while reading the story, then have the student read the story once again to build word recognition and fluency. The student should reread and master each story before progressing to the next one.

INSTRUCTOR SAYS – For this activity, you will spell eight **o** words that make the **short u** sound from the story. **The purpose of this exercise is for you to say each word you spell so slowly that you can hear each sound as you write each letter.**

Spell Advanced Short u Words from "Love"
love
son
young
moth-er
grand-moth-er
won-der
won-der-ful
does
broth-er
ton
smoth-er
oth-er
one (sounds like wun)

DURING THIS ACTIVITY – Cover the spelling words, so your student can't see them. Provide immediate feedback for correct responses with stars or happy faces. More importantly, provide immediate feedback for all errors by writing the correct word with a yellow marker and **ask the student to trace over each letter while saying its corresponding sound**.

 **EXPLAIN** – Look over all the words you spelled and trace over the letter **o** that make the **short u** sound with pink marker.

We've learned two ways we can spell the **short u** sound in the English language.

1) When the letter **u** is not on the end of a word or syllable

umbrella

2) The letter **a** on the end of a word or syllable

panda

CULTIVATING READING AND PHONICS SKILLS 1ST GRADE – 3RD GRADE

Spell Advanced Short u Spelling Patterns from "Love"

headline
armline
footline

a b c d e f g h i j k l m

n o p q r s t u v w x y z

STEP 8 | SUPPORT READING AND SPELLING WITH SOUND AWARENESS

> *You cannot plough a field by turning it over in your mind.*
>
> Gordon B. Hinckley

DEVELOP A RELATIONSHIP WITH THE PHONICS PATTERNS

When you meet people who are new or unfamiliar, it's easier to remember them if you've been formally introduced and then see them many times afterwards. Only then can you really start developing a relationship with them.

Similarly, when students have been formally introduced to phonics patterns and spelling conventions, they can develop their relationship with the letters and letter groups as well. Students need multiple exposures to orthographic phonic patterns by reading and spelling them again and again.

Make sure students don't just gloss over words they read and spell. Every day, students should take a few minutes to study and notice what words use which spelling patterns. If they do, then they will have more brain power to memorize words that do not follow patterns.

SHOW THE DIFFERENT WAYS WE SPELL THE SAME SOUND

We have learned that there are many ways we can spell sounds in the English language. For instance, the **long o** sound can be spelled **oa** or **ow**. Some words have **o** on the end of a syllable, like **yoyo**.

Instead of trying to remember the spelling of every single word, we now have the help of patterns for the majority of words in the English language.

CULTIVATING READING AND PHONICS SKILLS 1ST GRADE – 3RD GRADE

Consonant Spelling Patterns	
b	bird
c	cat
c	cereal
ch	chicken
ch	chemistry, Christmas
ck	duck
d	donut
f	fish
g	gum
g	giraffe
gh	laugh, tough
gh	thought, fought
h	hand
j	jar of jam
k	kite
kn	knee, knot
l	lion
m	monkey
n	napkin
p	pig
ph	phone
qu	quarter
r	rainbow
s	snake
sh	shell
t	tiger
th	three
v	van
w	watch
wh	whale, wheel
x	x-ray, box
y	yoyo
z	zebra
ci	musician, special
si	fusion, mission
ti	potion, position

Long Vowel Spelling Patterns		
Long Vowels on the End of Words and Syllables	a	a, cra-zy
	e	me, me-te-or
	i	hi, ti-ger
	o	no, pho-to
	u	men-u, mu-sic
Vowel Teams that Hold Hands	ai	rain
	ay	spray
	ea	beads
	ee	tree
	ey	key
	ie	pie
	oa	boat
	ue	blue glue
	ui	fruit juice
Vowel Teams that Jump Rope	a_e	cake
	e_e	gene
	i_e	bike
	o_e	hole
	u_e	mule
Advanced Long Vowel Spelling Patterns	ea	steak, great, break
	ey	hey! prey, convey
	ei	eight, weight
	ie	cookie
	i	ink, thing, Mississippi
	y	baby
	igh	night light
	y	butterfly
	ow	blowfish
	ol	goldfish
	ew	stew
	oo	moon

CULTIVATING READING AND PHONICS SKILLS 1ST GRADE – 3RD GRADE

Short Vowel Spelling Patterns		
Short Vowels	a	apple
	e	elephant
	i	igloo
	o	octopus
	u	umbrella
Advanced Short Vowel Spelling Patterns	a	panda
	a	spa
	au	laundry
	aw	straw
	al	chalk
	ea	feather
	o	love, mother, son
	y	gym, Egypt

The Other Vowel Spelling Patterns		
The Other Vowel Sounds	ow	cow
	ou	mouse
	oi	coin
	oy	boy
	oo	book
	ar	star
	or	fork
	ur	purple
	ir	shirt
	er	certificate

FREQUENTLY REVIEW ROUND UP WORDS

When students learn the different patterns in the structure of the English language, it will be easier for them to distinguish and remember words that do not follow patterns, like the words *said*, *buy*, and *there*.

During our sessions, if students didn't know how to read a word, then they might have written them down as a Round Up Word. Sometimes they may have been unsure if a word followed a phonics pattern. We may have written those words on their Round Up Paper. Now that we have learned almost all the patterns in the English language, we have a good idea which words follow a phonics pattern.

The following is an example of some words that students might have written on their Round Up Paper.

Common Round Up Words

of	are	been	could
two	come	said	should
to, into, onto	have	again	would
want	love	build	
was	some	buy	
what	there		
who			

Ask your student(s) to frequently read and spell the words on their Round Up Paper. Once they demonstrate mastery of words, you can cross out those words. Keep reviewing the unmastered words until all words are crossed out.

CONGRATULATIONS!

Congratulations on making it through the steps! Make sure that you take the time and energy to recognize your student(s) for their immense effort working towards mastery and autonomy. Everyone needs to feel valued for their effort and growth. Take time to share that they are more than just another person to you. Everyone needs to feel like they have purpose. How can you convey these truths to them? Keep the connection and have fun while you model what it means to be a good reader and human being. Take care!

CULTIVATING READING AND PHONICS SKILLS 1ST GRADE – 3RD GRADE

APPENDIX A: Beginning, Middle, End

APPENDIX B: 3-D Flash Cards
3-D Flash Cards: **Short Vowel Sounds**
Student colors letters with a **pink marker** then draws the keyword for each letter.

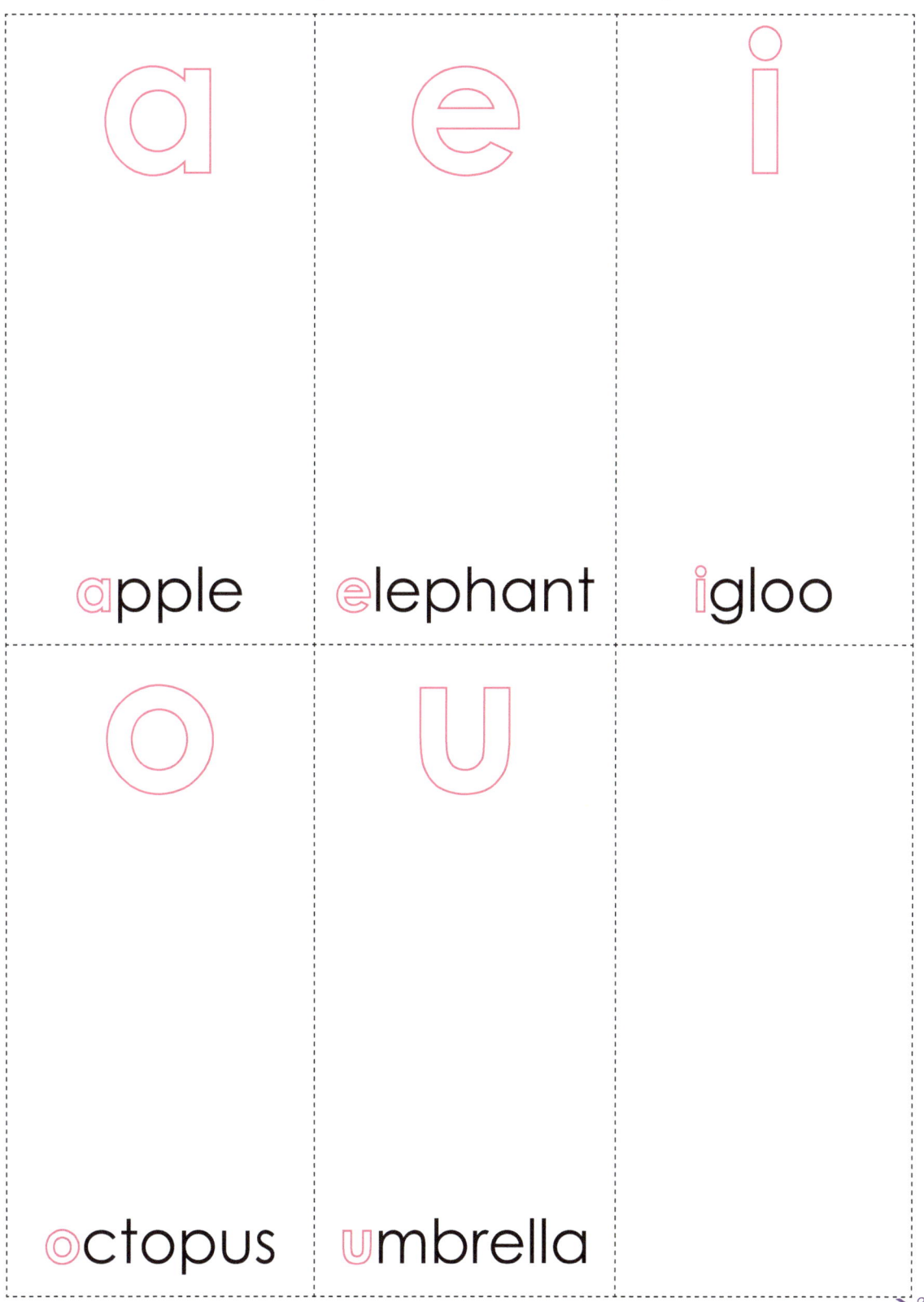

3-D Flash Cards: **Consonant Sounds**
Student colors letters with a **green marker** then draws the keyword for each letter.

c	s	r
cat	snake	rainbow
n	m	x
napkin	monkey	box

3-D Flash Cards: **Consonant Sounds**
Student colors letters with a **green marker** then draws the keyword for each letter.

3-D Flash Cards: **Consonant Sounds**
Student colors letters with a **green marker** then draws the keyword for each letter.

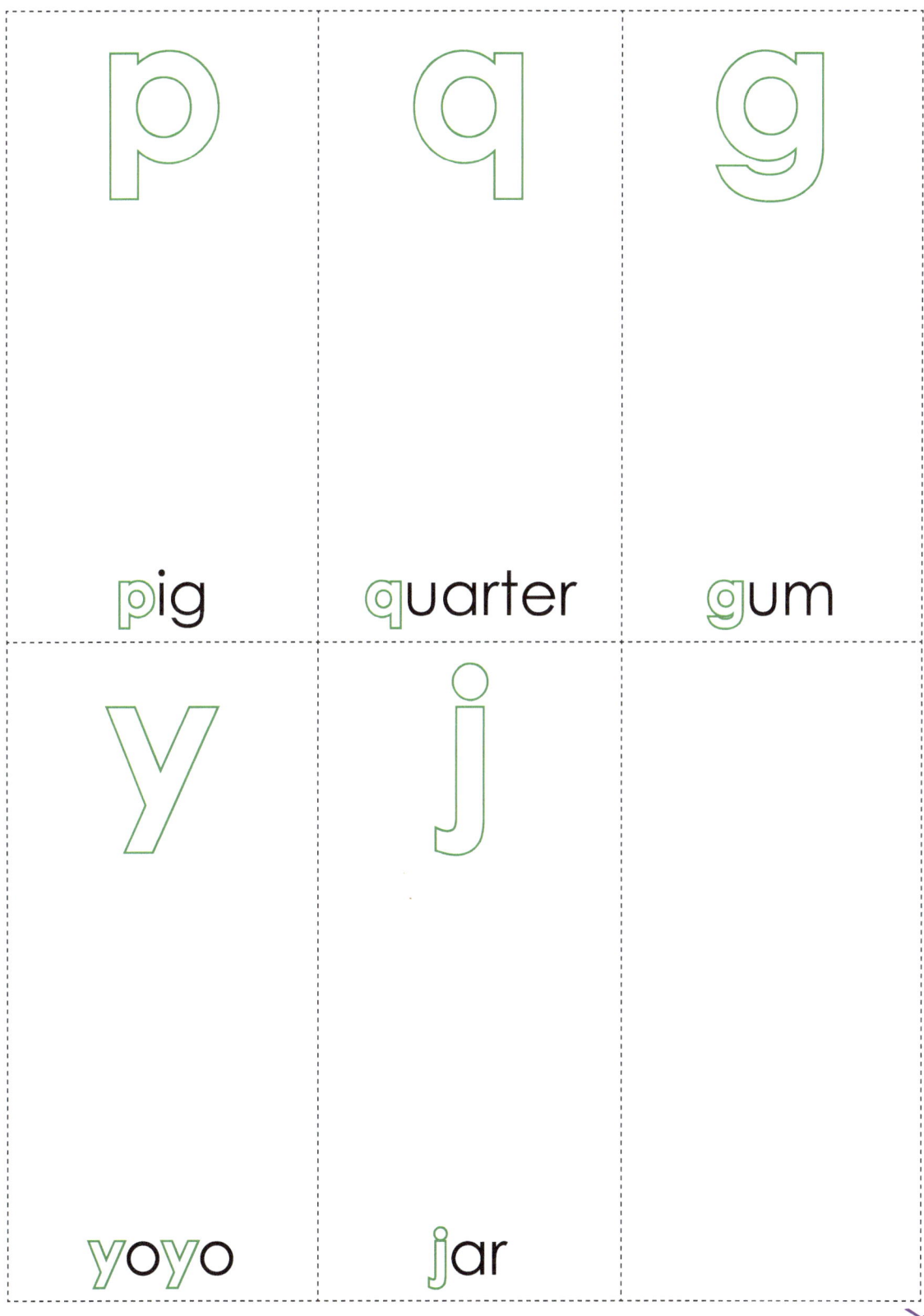

3-D Flash Cards: **Consonant Sounds**
Student colors letters with a **green marker** then draws the keyword for each letter.

3-D Flash Cards: **Consonant Sounds**
Student colors letters with a **green marker** then draws the keyword for each letter.

LAURIE HUNTER

3-D Flash Cards: **Consonant Sounds**
Student colors letters with a **green marker** then draws the keyword for each letter.

ch	sh	th
chicken	shell	three
ck	wh	
duck	whale	

3-D Flash Cards: **Long Vowel Sounds: Vowels on the End of Words and Syllables**
Student colors each letter with a **blue marker**.

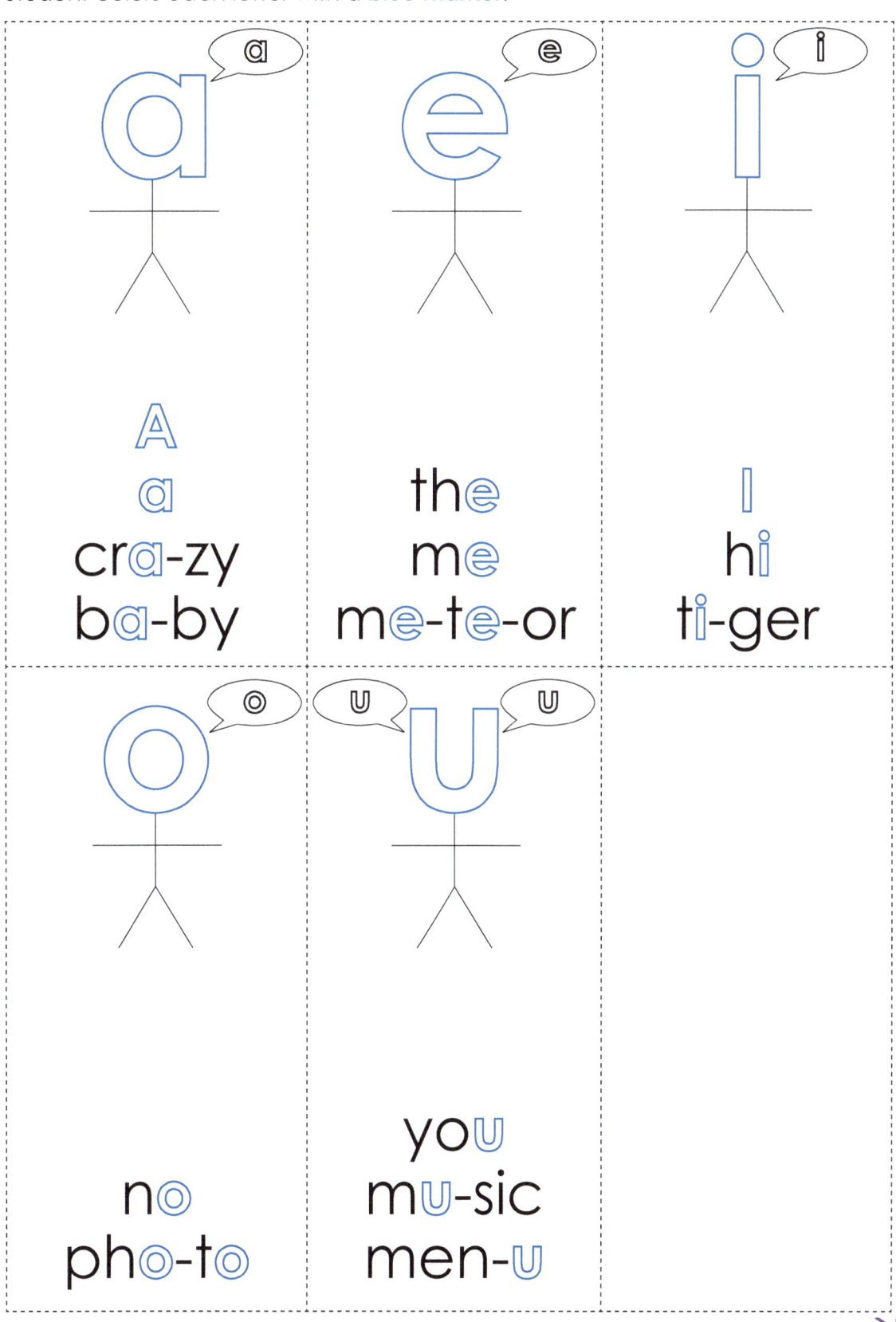

3-D Flash Cards: Long Vowel Sounds: Vowel Teams: ea ee ey ai ay oa ie ui ue
Student colors letter groups with a **blue marker** then draws the keyword for each card.

3-D Flash Cards: **Long Vowel Sounds: Vowel Teams: ea ee ey ai ay oa ie ui ue**
Student colors letter groups with a **blue marker** then draws the keyword for each card.

3-D Flash Cards: **Long Vowel Sounds: Vowel Teams: vowel-consonant-*silent e***
The student traces inside each outlined letter with a **blue marker** while saying each long vowel sounds.

3-D Flash Cards: **Consonant Sounds: Soft c and g**
The student colors the outlined letters with a **green marker**. Student does not need to draw the keyword for each letter.

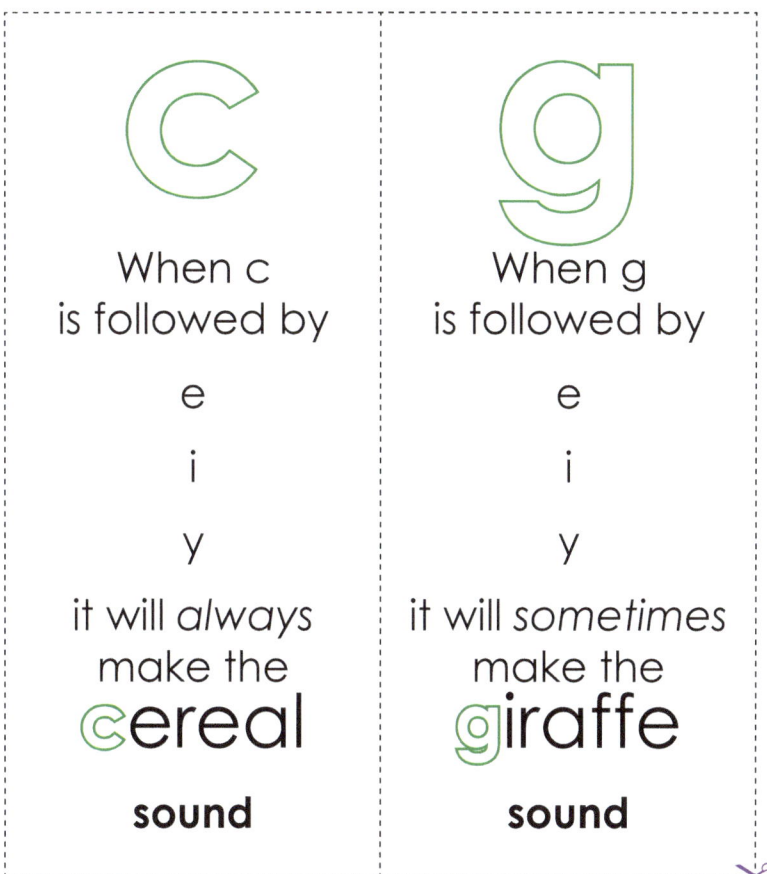

3-D Flash Cards: *The Other* Vowel Sounds: oi oy ow ou oo ar or ur ir er
Student colors letter groups with an orange marker then draws the keywords.

3-D Flash Cards: **The Other Vowel Sounds: oi oy ow ou oo ar or ur ir er**
Student colors letter groups with an **orange marker** then draws the keywords.

3-D Flash Cards: **Advanced Long Vowel Spelling Patterns: ie y igh y ow ol ew oo**
Student colors letter groups with a **blue marker** then draws the keyword for each card.

3-D Flash Cards: **Advanced Long Vowel Spelling Patterns: ie y igh y ow ol ew oo**
Student color groups letters with a **blue marker** then draws the keyword for each card.

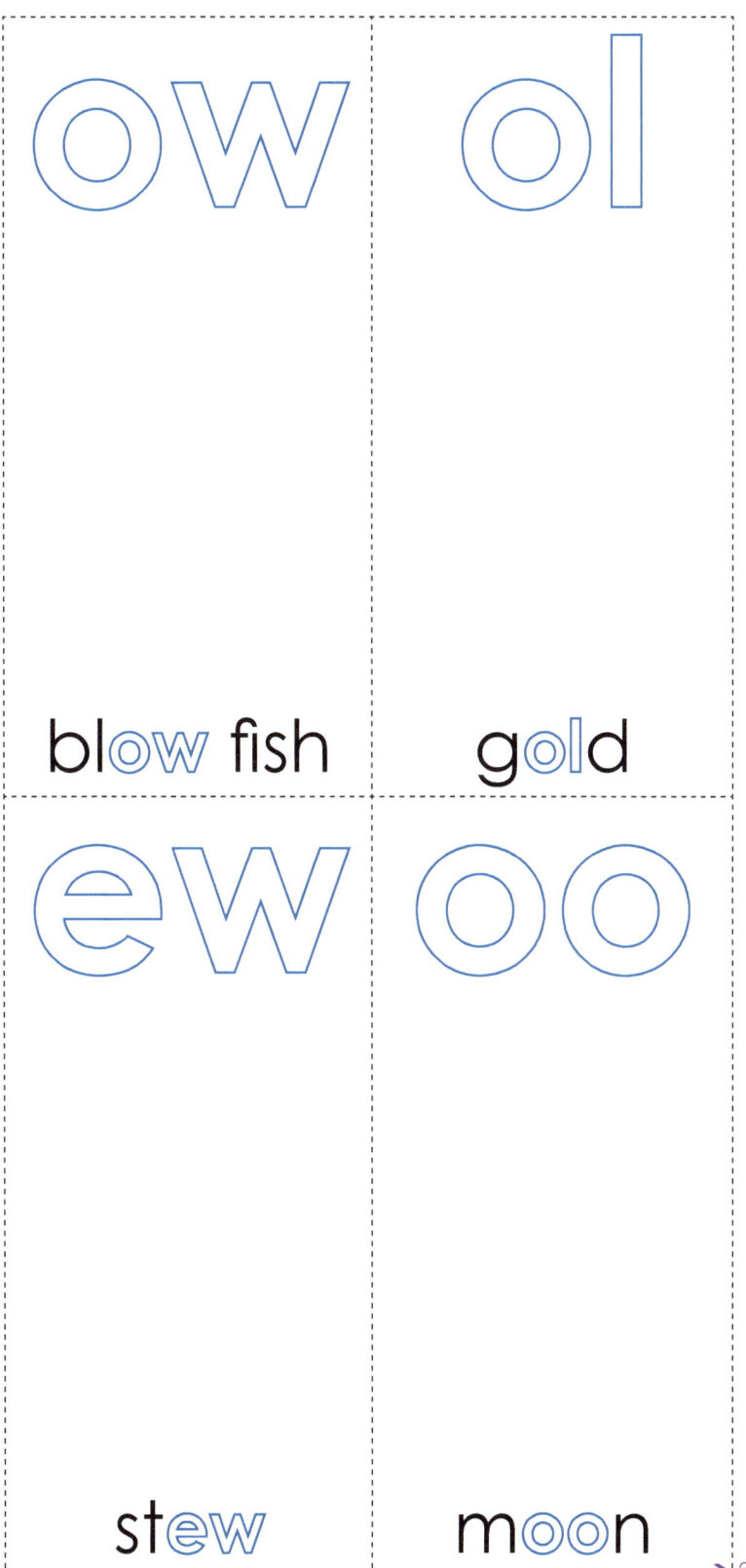

3-D Flash Cards: **Advanced Short Vowel Spelling Patterns: a a au aw al ea o y**
Student colors letter groups with **pink marker** then draws the keyword for each card.

3-D Flash Cards: **Advanced Short Vowel Spelling Patterns: a a au aw al ea o y**
Student colors letters with **pink marker** then draws the keyword for each letter (group).

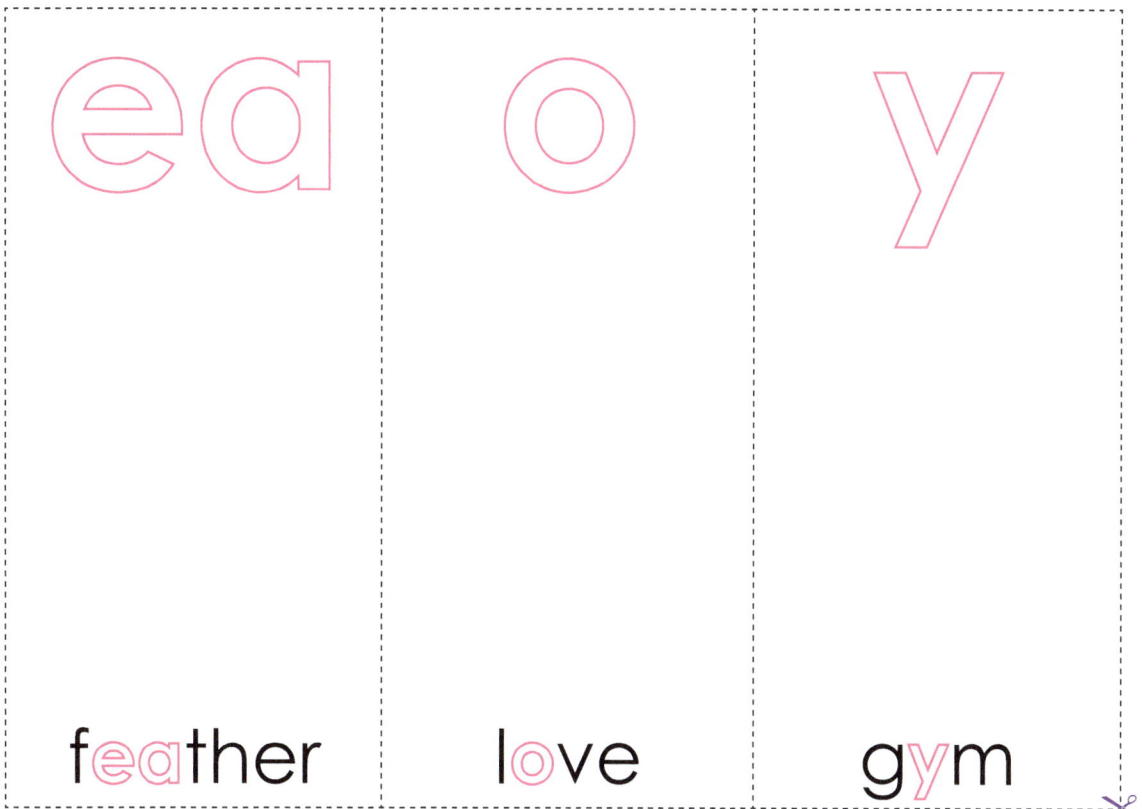

REFERENCES

Covey, S.R. (1989). *The 7 Habits of Highly Successful People.* New York, NY: Simon and Schuster.

Hallahan, (2005). *Learning Disabilities: Foundations, Characteristics, and Effective Teaching.* Boston, MA: Pearson.

Henshall, K. (1988). *A Guide to Remembering Japanese Characters.* Tokyo: Charles E. Tuttle Company, Inc.

Hinckley, G (1996, September 22). *A conversation with single adults.* [Conference presentation]. Salt Lake, UT.

Holmes, O. (1858). *The Autocrat of the Breakfast Table.* Cambridge, MA: Riverside Press.

Hunter, L. (2004, 2005). *Mosaic Reading.* Austin, TX: Self-published instruction manual..

Hunter, L. (2008). *Evaluating the Impact of an Intervention on Struggling Readers.* The University of Texas at Austin, TX: Master's Thesis.

Mercer & Campbell. (1997). *Great Leaps Reading.* Gainesville, FL: Diarmuid, Inc.

National Reading Panel (2000). *Teaching children to read: An evidence-based assessment of the scientific research literature on reading and its implications for reading instruction.* Washington, DC: National Institute of Child Health and Human Development.

Rayner, K., Foorman, B., Perfetti, C., Pesetsky, D., & Seidenberg, M. (2001). How psychological science informs the teaching of reading. *Psychological Science in the Public Interest,* 2(2), Nov, 31-74.

Richards, R. (1999). *The Source for Dyslexia and Dysgraphia.* East Moline, IL: Linguisystems, Inc.

Wilson, B. (2002). *Wilson Reading System Instructor Manual, 3rd Edition.* Milbury, MA: Wilson Language Training.

World Food Program USA. (2020, June 22). *History's hunger heroes: Etharin Cousin.*

www.ingramcontent.com/pod-product-compliance
Lightning Source LLC
Chambersburg PA
CBHW042129010526
44111CB00031B/37